Halal حلال
Branding

To Maria

Halal حلال
Branding
JONATHAN A.J. WILSON PHD

It was a pleasure
having you as a
Marketing Student,
d seeing you grow
as a professional has
been so cool !!

1 2 3 4 5 6 7 8 9 10

CLARITAS BOOKS

Bernard Street, Swansea, United Kingdom
Milpitas, California, United States

© CLARITAS BOOKS 2018

First Published in September 2018

Typeset in Helvetica 12/14
Printed by Mega Basim Printing in Turkey

Halal Branding
By Prof. Jonathan A. J. Wilson PhD
Cover design by Dragonfly Black

A CIP catalogue record for this book is available from the British Library

ISBN: 978-1-905837-57-1

DEDICATION

I dedicate this book to my Creator - as a labour of love and honest attempt to do the best that I can with what I've got.

I also dedicate this work to my supersmart Wife who's sharpened me, and my two superstar Daughters.

Blessings and thanks to my superfly business partner Mohamed Geraldez and our team at Dragonfly Black.

Finally, hugs to my Father and little Brother, and prayers to my sorely missed Mother and paternal Grandmother.

...And anyone else that knows me – know that you're not forgotten and I am a reflection of you!

Professor Jonathan A.J. Wilson PhD is an award-winning Academic and Partner of the Business and Brand Strategy firm, Dragonfly Black. He has spent the past 20 years specialising in what he calls the ABCDs of Business and culture: Advertising, Branding, Communications, and Digital. With a Chemistry degree, MBA and PhD in Branding, he champions the art in Science and the science in Art.

Professor Wilson has published over 200 pieces of work, which have led to over 100 conference-speaking engagements across the globe.

He has developed a reputation for being an electric, insightful and quick-witted public speaker able to tackle real-world trending phenomena. Professor Wilson has worked internationally with a range of government, organisation, and university clients on projects in the following industry sectors: Halal, travel, tourism, education, technology, media, food, fashion, cosmetics, pharmaceuticals, finance, professional services, music, and sports. Also, he flies in to deliver corporate in-house training regularly - either through Dragonfly Black, or as a professional trainer for Al Jazeera Media Network in Qatar.

Professor Wilson's research papers and articles on Halal Branding and Muslim Pop Culture are some of the most widely cited globally - with his recent work on Egyptian Muslim Millennials post Arab Spring receiving an award. Away from Halal, Professor Wilson has received awards for his research on Sports Branding, Leadership Training across cultures, and Luxury Branding. His published research on Luxury Branding and Inconspicuous Consumption won Best-Paper in the Journal of Marketing Management and appeared in the Harvard Business Review.

At the end of 2017, he received a LinkedIn Top Voices Award, where he was praised for his edgy commentary and insight into Intersectionality, Future Trends, Personal Branding, and Student Engagement. Professor Wilson was also one of the featured professionals in LinkedIn's cross-platform advertising campaigns – something that he is especially proud of, as he was the only UK academic.

www.dragonflyblack.com
www.drjonwilson.com
@drjonwilson

www.halalbranding.com
www.islamicbranding.com

FORWARD

Many moons ago, I recall an evening where I first saw a famous fast food restaurant that will remain unnamed "attempt" to message to a specific group of diverse consumers that they had not tried to connect with previously. I remember being shocked at how poorly it was executed— and thought to myself, "wow, they really should have done a better job understanding that identity and that culture before they attempted to link their product and brand to that identity!" As a researcher deeply intrigued by both branding and identity for the last twenty-five years of my academic career, I am always on the lookout for provocative and intellectually stimulating discourse that can help myriad folks interested in speaking to culturally diverse audiences, "not screw it up." I try to read voraciously, and it is always a delight when I come across a rare gem that is both academically engaging, practical and timely on these sorts of issues.

Halal Branding by Jonathan A.J. Wilson is such a book. Jon is an inwardly unique blend of charismatic, thoughtful and intellectual clarity—outwardly displayed in a flamboyant, tirelessly energetic pair of pink shoes. I was introduced to him through his research, and invited him to join me on my weekly Wharton Pod Cast on Sirius XM channel 111 "Marketing Matters." It was at that moment that I succinctly realized that even though we come from different worlds, we share a collective passion for learning, Hip Hop, branding and real talk. Hence, I was excited to get a gander at his book. Jon warmly invites the reader to become a kindred spirit, and strips away the technical jargon in order to get to the heart of the matter: To identify the absolute key issues in the goal of undertaking, robust and authentic Halal branding efforts. He advises but robustly pushes the reader outside of their comfort zone, to tackle deep but important areas of understanding, in a mosaic of thought interspersed with case studies, humor and intellectual depth.

Religion may have been the very first "brand", and so thinking about brand not as simply a collection of colors and logos, but as a complex, and strategically constructed meaning system can add value to an asset you are trying to create. Doing so in the context of pop cultural and socio-political change is doubly hard. In *Halal Branding*, Jon artfully takes the reader end to end not only on a journey of both intellectual discovery, but thoughtful and provocative practical insight and action steps—as he encourages the reader to rethink brand theory through his unique intellectual lens. As he correctly suggests, researchers, advertising professionals, entrepreneurs, students and conscious consumers who seek to better understand the what, the when and how of Halal branding will appreciate this book and as these eight chapters will serve as an important guide to make sure that you "get it right."

Professor Americus Reed, II

The Wharton School, University of Pennsylvania, Philadelphia USA

Professor Reed is the Wharton School's only 'Brand Identity Theorist', and The Whitney M. Young Jr. Professor of Marketing - receiving his PhD from the University of Florida, and his MS and BA degrees from Georgia State University. His research focuses on brand identity loyalty and the role consumers' self-concepts play in guiding buying decisions. He examines how social identity, social influence, values, attitudes and judgments interact in shaping purchase decisions and consumer behavior.

CONTENTS

WHAT THE HALAL IS GOING ON?!

CHAPTER ONE:

WHAT THE HALAL IS GOING ON?!

I think it is important to begin a book of this nature, which essentially is both a window and instructional guide into *Halal Branding* with my ontological and epistemological positions. In plain English, that means my worldview, position, or starting point, and how I gather knowledge and put it into practice. Those are the: *who, what, how, where, when,* and *why* questions. Or even more practically: so what, what now, and what can we do about it?

It would be easy for me to write yet another book on the technical and Sharia aspects of classifying and certifying something Halal; or a narrative on the pillars of Islam and anecdotes reporting the different clusters of Muslims present today. However, from my experiences, this information doesn't necessarily equip you with the ability to create winning brands.

All too often, discussions on Halal focus on permissibility and compliance - and they are championed by Halal certifiers, religious clergy, sociologists and journalists. They lead you to the doorstep of the market, by raising a flag and citing large numerically based market potential data - but less is said about how you can walk through the door and dominate the market. At times, I'd even go as far to say that in presenting Halal's uniqueness it reinforces a sense of alienation that hampers the overall objective of Halal, which ultimately is to go mainstream.

What people frequently ask me to comment on is how to market and brand Halal and its associated products and services. Therefore, the contents of this book have been designed to address these pain points and offer a practical roadmap towards brand building.

I've also not wanted to localise the book too much by examining particular regions. Whilst Muslims are united by one faith, other factors such as religiosity, age, culture, nationality, sector, technology acceptance, education, current affairs etc can have a significant impact on Brand Strategy. Having made this point, I am however confident that using the toolkits in this book can deliver measurable differences in this space.

Therefore, the purpose of this book is to provide an academic and theoretical foundation, which is grounded in practical case studies, but ultimately is intended to assist and encourage scholars and practitioners in their under-standing and engagement within the modern Halal space.

Whether you are a student; researcher; entrepreneur; small business owner; corporate; professional in advertising, branding, marketing, and public relations; or even a con-scious consumer - this has been written with you all in mind.

I believe that this book fills a gap, where beyond media

WHAT THE HALAL?!

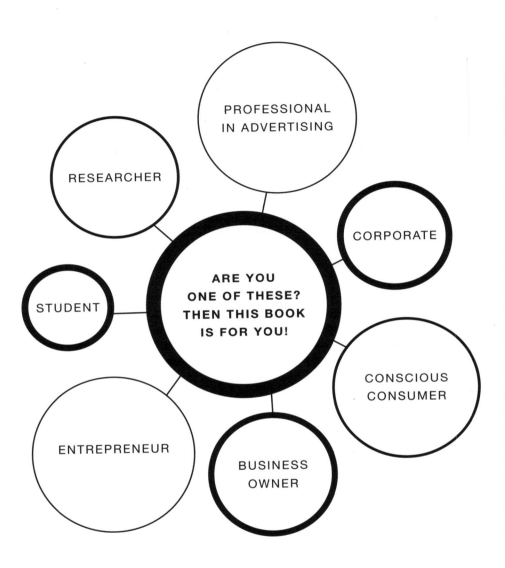

pieces that announce and cheerlead the potential of Halal; and relative to the size of the markets, the global audiences, and its future potential, there are few sources of information available that deep dive into how things look and can grow.

In previous talks and articles I've joked about Halal being more than 'meat and money'. Perhaps in fact it's about 'meat, money, marriage, Muhammad (peace be upon him), and Mecca' …but definitely Muslims and non-Muslims today are often left wondering *'what the Halal is going on?'*

With this in mind, this book is intended to bridge that divide and bring together bodies of information that examine: Islam in historical and contemporary contexts; Muslim majority and minority geographies; the intersectionality of slow and fast cultures; emerging markets; geopolitical factors; business innovation and industrialisation; behavioural economics consumption and consumer psychology – and ultimately Branding as the vehicle to galvanize and bring these elements together, in order to develop commercial, economic and societal value.

This is something that I have described as bringing to life the *'Spirit of Spirituality'* and *'Profiting from Prophethood'*.

I'd like to take a moment to answer some of the common questions I've received over the years, which will help to frame discussions. Essentially they can be grouped into the need to establish two factors: Understanding, and Controlling.

Firstly, I believe that what we are experiencing is a completely new phenomenon, for reasons that I will explain later - and therefore this new 'Halal' reality is something that we are experiencing for the first time.

However, few understand it fully, nor do many have all the answers for what it is and does in the here and now – that is the nature of phenomena! Also, this is largely because this is a field that requires expertise and exposure to a vast number of subject disciplines, industries, and regions, and things are moving quickly and at scale.

I would say that it's unusual for a branding, advertising and marketing professional to sit with Sharia scholars and Halal certifiers; sift through and peer review hundreds of academic journal articles; watch abattoir slaughter video footage; visit DNA lab testing food laboratories; visit dozens of countries frequently attending conferences on food, fashion, finance, tourism, tech, and religion; undertake ethnographic studies; attempt to learn new languages; and even slaughter a cow in a village in Malaysia – just to get an handle on *what the Halal is going on* and just to be able to do branding, advertising, and marketing… but this is something that I'm proud to say that I have done. It has become my labour of love, and has been an essential aspect of me trying to understand the Halal phenomenon.

Secondly, linked to this, these questions are a basis for establishing philosophical, conceptual, and practical arguments, which then also influence how the field develops, which are essential due to the number of stakeholders involved and what is at stake.

Therefore, my aim in the rest of this chapter is to establish some underpinning principles and arguments that set out my approach to this discipline - based upon some ten years of research, writing, speaking, and working on brands in the Halal space.

HALAL IS MORE THAN 'MEAT AND MONEY'

THE RACE TO CLEAR THOSE HALAL HURDLES

So it's official – everyone wants a piece of the Halal action. If it's for rewards in the hereafter, or revenue generation in the here and now: achieving Halal status is something that many businesses are exploring.

Halal, as a means for delivering competitive advantage, is considered to be an *x-factor* - which can help to expand operations, create new markets and draw in more consumers. In the shadow of the economic downturn, Halal has also been able to increase brand value, relieve constraints associated with barriers to entry, and stabilize fluctuating markets.

Muslims, like other ethnic segments, such as the Afro-American Market, are seen to exhibit stronger signs of loyalty trans-nationally, which in some cases have acted as a catalyst to draw in wider non-Muslim communities. From this, it can be argued that Halal presents an adaptation of existing management and brand thinking. The interesting phenomenon spearheading this now, is that the concept and nature of Halal, warrants verification which is supported by overt branding practices.

Traditionally, Halal was largely held to be self-evident, through the idea that the majority of things are Halal, according to the Qur'an. Where matters necessitated further investigation, conclusions were rarely derived from branding.

Instead, an assessment of Halal arose from examining ingredients, the environment and the involved individuals. However, with so many products and services on the market, from so many sources, it is inevitable that branding becomes of more significance. Brands are conspicuous - they differentiate, inform and reassure.

Furthermore, whilst it could be argued that Muslim minority and non-Muslim nations should have a greater need for such labeling and reassurances: in fact, this trend also extends to Muslim nations and Muslim majority populations. Halal fever has gripped the psyche of the Muslim consumer and it could be argued that businesses are also reaping the rewards of Muslim piety and risk aversion.

So much so, that *Halal* as a descriptor is being used for more and more commodities, services and activities. Without looking at simply 'meat and money', Halal is even being used to describe, amongst other things: milk, water, drugs, holidays, washing powder, tissues, socks, websites, music – you name it and they'll label and brand it!

HALAL AS A DESCRIPTOR IS BEING USED FOR

 TISSUES

 MILK

 WATER

 DRUGS

MUSIC

KEY QUESTIONS CONCERNING HALAL BUSINESS

The following questions are ones that other businesses and I frequently face and consider:

- How does *Halal* 'fit' into the branding world, if at all?
- What branding approaches work and can be used?
- How much knowledge and how many practitioners exist, with sufficient cross-functional skills, to champion both the Halal and Branding?
- Who sets the agenda?
- How can Halal Marketing and Branding move forward?

The race has started, but rather than there being a clear finishing line ahead, in many cases it appears that the finishing tape looks more like rows of red tape. The following section considers these questions and takes a look at some of the challenges being faced currently.

WHAT THE HALAL IS GOING ON?!

HALAL IS CONSIDERED TO BE AN **X-FACTOR** - WHICH CAN HELP TO EXPAND OPERATIONS, CREATE NEW MARKETS AND DRAW IN MORE CONSUMERS.

HURDLE NO.1: *HALAL* IN ITSELF IS NOT A BRAND

Many discussions and practices talk of Halal being a brand – it's not! Also, what is Halal branding – does that mean branding in a Halal way, or a brand that identifies a product or service as comprising of Halal components?

Halal is a descriptor and therefore can be termed an *Ingredient* Brand, but on it's own it definitely isn't a brand. Ordinarily, within branding this wouldn't be so much of a problem, as we can see *Fair Trade, Suitable for Vegetarians, Sugar Free, Organic* and other ingredient brand labels.

However, Halal is more than a brand. Its meaning in some ways is being constricted by the constraints of current brand theoretical understandings - which focus on classification, identification and economic drivers.

As will be discussed later, brands are far richer and more organic in their essence. A strong argument therefore can be made instead for a classification, which says *Suitable for Muslims*, as this allows for more emotive traits.

Also, there are already concerns that some products such as sweets, or noodles containing MSG (Monosodium Glutamate – a flavour enhancer) are technically Halal, but the idea that they are linked to spiritual purity, health and goodness (which Halal professes) poses problems in the minds of some consumers.

As an extension of this concept, it would be interesting to see how consumers would respond if more luxury goods and high fashion choose to adopt Halal labeling for their products. Philosophically, an argument can be made for Halal encompassing all of these commodities, but does such conspicuous consumption and consumerism sit well with Islamic ideals, which encourage control and moderation of the *nafs* (self)?

HURDLE NO.2: WHO CERTIFIES WHAT IS HALAL?

If an increasing number of products are being classified as being Halal through labeling, who and how should this process be controlled? Are they specifically a religious, scientific, governmental, societal, or business issue – or more generally, a collective responsibility?

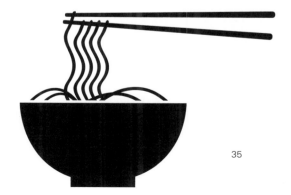

If these issues are not addressed, then the knock-on effect is fivefold:

1. Perceptions of what is Halal have the potential to be distorted, to the detriment of Islam and Muslims
2. Businesses may be hindered unnecessarily in their ability to market products
3. Consumer cynicism may lead to the mistrust of certain Halal products, without reason
4. The term *Halal* may lose its sparkle and become worn out, in much the same way as many affordable and widely available products being branded *Luxury*
5. Perhaps even worse, businesses could set the agenda on defining a core aspect of Islamic beliefs and practices.

Collectively, also current trends are leading to a worrying practice where more *Halal* ingredient brands and certifying bodies are being continually launched. This can already be observed with some products, carrying more than one Halal label. I remember seeing one brand of powdered milk, sold in Malaysia, carrying two Halal labels: one Malaysian and one Thai. It could even be argued, from a traditional religious perspective, whether there is an inherent need for even one Halal label?!

THE **5** HURDLES FOR HALAL BRANDING

---

1 HALAL IS NOT A BRAND, BUT CAN BE BRANDED

2 WHO CERTIFIES WHAT IS HALAL?

3 SOCIAL AND BRANDING RESPONSIBILITIES

4 A GOOD BRAND IS NOT ONLY YOUR FRIEND, BUT ALSO HUMAN

5 VALUE BRANDS, OR VALUE FOR MONEY?

6 HALAL FOR LIFE, AND HALAL ON A LARGE SCALE

Marketers and politicians alike would most likely argue in favour of this practice, as it offers, control, financial and strategic gains. However, we return to the same point – *Halal* offers much more to humanity.

Why I argue that this is worrying, is because too many labels raise problems in the same way that too few labels does – distractions from core issues, barriers and restrictive business practices. So there has to be a balance and I think that we have yet to reach a happy equilibrium.

HURDLE NO.3: SOCIAL AND BRANDING RESPONSIBILITIES

Muslims, whilst wanting to minimize risks in decision-making through making safe and informed judgments, aren't afraid to express their views! Single-issue politics groups, tactical boycotting, social networking, word of mouth and cultural diversity, all are important elements in the lives of modern Muslim consumers. The challenges posed by this, are that businesses are attempting to market to passionate consumers, who largely seek conformity of consumption, but don't necessarily consume in the same way, have strong cultural views and don't like to be told what to do.

Because of this, I am not so convinced of there being one homogenous Global Muslim Millennial segment for example. On the face of it, the argument appears to make sense – but if we dig deeper, I think that it would be superficial to assume that such wide audiences all consume exactly for the same reason, in the same way, and derive the same feelings. Just like any other consumer segments, Muslims are dynamic, nuanced, culturally influenced, and at times unpredictable.

In contrast, if we look to iconic global brands, the best branding at some stage looks to take risks – in order to differentiate a brand from the pack. Therefore, it's worth considering how Muslim brand professionals are able to take the reigns, offer balance and set the agenda. All too often, in the face of interest but uncertainty, Halal brands play it safe, for fear of failure or causing offence.

The market can be grouped largely into two areas: conventional brands that seek Halal labeling, and *Born Halal* brands that sadly have a tendency towards copying existing brands, with minor ingredient, cosmetic and name adjustments.

To save the face of any existing products, I'll illustrate my point with a fictitious example: The *Namaz* chocolate bar, which *"helps you work, rest and pray"* [think of the *Mars* bar (which does exist), with the strapline: "A Mars a day, helps you work, rest and play"]. Rather than marketing driving exponential growth of creativity, it's recycling the same ideas

- which will eventually lead to a decline in innovation.

These occurrences often also lead to consumer cognitive dissonance in many instances and are perhaps some of the many reasons why Muslim companies find it difficult to maintain a long-term competitive position. Namely: many brands looking to target Muslims take less risks and restrict creative innovation – maybe through lack of knowledge, or to avoid censure.

The pressure becomes further compounded by the fact that adding the term *Halal* now invites consumers to become religious judges and juries. Because, effectively Halal labeling doesn't just mean permissibility, it also says that the product, service and producer are producing something religiously pure. And, because they are branded as such, products or services could be judged and scrutinized to a greater degree, continuously.

HURDLE NO.4: A GOOD BRAND IS NOT ONLY YOUR FRIEND, BUT ALSO HUMAN

Brand practitioners and academics will tell you that humans are more emotional than rational. Following this, brands work best when they appeal to our emotional sides. Therefore, good brands are those that are as life-like as you can get them. They not only have identities, but also have com-

MUSLIMS ARE
DYNAMIC,
NUANCED,
CULTURALLY
INFLUENCED,
AND AT TIMES
UNPREDICTABLE

plicated personalities, they seek meaningful relationships with us - and these are beyond financial calculations. After all, how easy is it to put a price on a friendship?

With this in mind, brands are vulnerable and fallible, just like humans. So a key question is are Islamic or Halal brands making a rod for their own back, because they are making claims that are almost impossible to live up to?

Perhaps a better model would be for brands to aim to create an existence that profiles them as a Muslim. We all know Muslims make mistakes from time to time and we are ready to accept and forgive. Therefore, brands may achieve further acceptance and authenticity through: not preaching so much, relaying more stories connected with their own purpose and existence, making use of other emotions such as humour and compassion.

This is perhaps also why some non-Muslim brands fare well when they decide to target Muslims at a later date, because they have first invested in relaying a wider range of human emotions.

HURDLE NO.5: VALUE BRANDS, OR VALUE FOR MONEY?

The Halal market appears to centre on attempting the impossible goal of delivering: a valued brand, with the best of values, which is value for money, and for less money.

An underlying feeling exists, both from consumers and some Muslim business, which suggests that charging a premium is wrong and may not be received well by the market. One sales pitch being that *born Halal* brands do not overcharge and exploit consumers.

The argument here is that this approach restricts the necessary revenue required to build a brand and its market potential. Furthermore, this may hamper a business when attempting to compete on a level playing field - compared with other conventional marketing models.

An example of this can be seen with some Muslim-owned television stations, which rely on charitable donations and are unable to then generate sufficient revenue through advertising. The eventual conclusions being that the product line declines (not due to demand), or cost measures have to be implemented, which reduce the quality of materials and working conditions. They simply don't have the money to promote their offerings or brand build, which are essential components to growing your audience and reputation building. Also, it leaves them open to more established and mainstream media companies - who can pivot and steal audiences, with their stronger brands and wider reach. Markets and businesses more so than ever today are Brand-driven and Marketing-orientated. If you build your brand, then you can charge more and that opens up more opportunities.

To undo such market dynamics and perceptions will take time and education – but ultimately this can be achieved through brand building, marketing communications and customer relationship marketing (which of course require investment and skilled execution).

HURDLE NO.6: HALAL FOR LIFE, AND HALAL ON A LARGE SCALE

It is worth considering how brands are able to maintain their Halal credentials. For example, if an organization at a later stage is found to be engaging in practices, which are deemed to be incompatible with Halal ideals, beyond ingredients: such as running sweatshops and bad management practices - what happens now?

Of course the argument should be that their Halal status should be challenged. However, it is questionable whether the mechanisms are in place to regulate these aspects.

On the same line, another area worthy of consideration, is at what level of output do manufacture, production and services begin to diminish in achieving Halal exemplars of best practice? It may be possible to certify, then deliver

Halal products and services in the beginning - but when demand increases, should a limit be proposed, which is dictated by Halal ideas, rather than economies of scale?

SO HOW CAN WE REACH THE FINISHING LINE?

For the reasons stated, and as a core facet of human nature, it is unlikely that all Muslims will ever be able to agree on one approach to *Halal Branding*. Debates continue to run over matters such as the stunning of animals prior to slaughter, the use of alcohol in fragrances, and even philosophical arguments against labeling alcohol free beers.

My position is that these consultation processes and such opinion sharing, should be welcomed - but it should also be assumed that they will carry on indefinitely. Therefore, stakeholders should be encouraged to consider that seeking complete control and consensus are divisive and energy sapping.

So, whilst in theory it is possible to discern what is Halal and what is not; when something seeks to carry branding and certification, this becomes more difficult to evaluate.

MUSLIMS AS THE NEW EXOTICA

The following are some suggestions of areas that could be explored in the future:

- Further discussions surrounding the unification of certification practices and certifiers.
- The role of country of origin and nation branding in communicating brand value.
- Think tanks, comprising of religious scholars and brand experts, across schools of thought and market sectors.
- Formal consumer-led watchdog groups, using social media.
- Expansion and separation of Halal classifications. These could be used to differentiate between products, which are technically Halal and those that have additional benefits, associated with health and nutritional values – as a sort of traffic light system. So for example, some products could achieve Halal status, whilst others achieve a label classifying them as being *Suitable for Muslims.* In addition, scaling systems could be provided which indicate how much consumption is recommended.
- A labeling system and marketing communications approach, which allow for ease of understanding by non-Muslims. And, beyond this, it has the potential to evoke similar positive traits. After all, Islamic thought

would argue that Halal resonates with all human spirits, regardless of their current belief systems - as all are created with the potential to understand, by Allah. However, there still appears to be a paucity of understanding by the wider community, as to what Halal covers - other than 'meat and money'.

- Specific academic courses which focus on Muslim Consumer Behaviour and Islamic Branding.
- Further research into how brand theories can be used in an Islamic context, allowing for further application of cognitive behavioural psychology, to elicit the more emotional attributes of a brand, without going against the ideals of Islam. Following this, attempts could be made to launch emotive premium high-end luxury brands.

DEFINING HALAL BRANDS AND BRANDING
What is a Halal Brand?

I will be going into some more detail later as to what categorizes something as being *Halal*, but as I have stated: the basic principle is that Halal means a permissible commodity or action, according to the rules and teachings as outlined in Islam.

Similarly, I will define and outline later what constitutes a Brand, but at this stage we should consider that:

WHAT THE HALAL IS GOING ON?!

A *Halal Brand*, signals the decision to both strategically and overtly: position, signal, and communicate a branded commodity aligned with the values, norms, and ideals of the Muslim faithful.

Some may question why I have decided to explain *Halal* according to Islam, and ascribe *Halal branding* to Muslims. My reasoning is that ultimately, brands are judged according to their performance in the market, and acceptance by consumers and wider stakeholders. It is of little use to discuss the creation of a brand theoretically, if practically it is not able to deliver its core functions of: added recognition, value, and trust. These will be judged by humans, who cross-reference their decisions with their understanding and intentions linked to the rules and teachings of Islam.

This for me is an important guiding principle, because I have listened to other practitioners and scholars who have encountered difficulties in trying to explain and justify various approaches, or decide what terms to use. These have lead people to debate whether they should or can use terms such as: Islamic Branding, Islamic Marketing, Muslim friendly, Sharia compliant, and even perversely Sharia friendly! These debates are likely to continue...

Beyond grabbing media headlines, or making agency pitches and conference talks, I believe that few have been able to articulate clearly what makes any of these new 'branded' approaches conceptually different. Rather, they present a monolithic definition of mainstream Branding and Marketing (which at times is negative), and then offer an ethnocentric alternative, as a panacea (which at times is politically charged) - but one however that largely follows the same existing guiding principles, with little disruption.

What I present in this book is a branding approach that is the culmination of my PhD findings in Global Branding and Culture, in which I investigated: Eastern and Western perspectives of slow and fast culture, philosophy and spirituality; key historical, technological, sociological, and geopolitical events; and the views of industry experts.

Therefore, on one level you could just read this as being another book on branding that is applicable to all - and is rooted in principles derived from Islamic civilizations, instead of drawing from Western Christian thought, as is often the case elsewhere.

I argue that Christianity features heavily in much branding, because the vast majority of top brands, scholars, and literature hail from the (Christian) West, or are educated in the West and use terms such as *icons* - and therefore view branding through a Western Christian lens. Not to say that this is wrong, but it is debatable whether Halal Brands, or

I JOKED: THESE HALAL CERTIFIERS ARE ALWAYS ARGUING OVER STUNNING CHICKS

brands from other Muslim-centric cultures can achieve their full potential by following this path.

The alternative position that I am presenting here is that within this book: the following reference base, blend of models and approach are designed to increase your likelihood of presenting an authentic branding offering that will perform better in Muslim minority and majority markets.

For that to occur, *Halal Branding*, conceptually, strategically, and practically puts you in a much stronger position than conventional Branding and Marketing, or Islamic Branding and Marketing, or Sharia certification approaches currently have been able to achieve.

I believe this because Halal is clearly understood to be about lived everyday experiences linked to consumption, faith, and societal interactions with Muslims and non-Muslims. It is a bottom-up approach, which deals with those day-to-day decisions that people make about the little things. Following these, the bigger Islamic position or Muslim identity issues can be served and addressed.

The strength of this way of thinking is that it provides practical answers in preference to what may be abstract, political, evangelical, or propaganda infused instructions. This is not to say that Halal hasn't faced these challenges, but ultimately Halal is a component of Islam, and at times when the term Islamic has been applied to low involvement commodities it seems a stretch too far or trivialisation of a belief system.

The terms *Islamic* or *Sharia* bring into question how the sacred, mundane and profane can be linked credibly to these terms without attracting censure. They also at times elicit negative connotations, fear, and raise discussions as to the role of non-Muslims as providers or consumers. But the absence of any reference or link to Islam leaves a gap in what now has been viewed as a multi-trillion dollar opportunity to a multi-billion population audience.

WHAT IS HALAL BRANDING?

Halal Branding is the active process of delivering the promise presented by the Halal Branded offering - raising desire, elevating its status and reputation. Whilst both are linked, for me there is a subtle difference between creating a *Halal Brand* and undertaking *Halal Branding*. Both are ultimately judged by actions and intentions.

However, depending on the company and commodity, you may choose to be more or less overt on the various brand elements, such as: product design, package design, name, logo, Halal certification, country or origin, founder and employer branding, promotional activities, and place of sale.

Therefore, what I am saying is that you can create a strong and overt Halal Brand and at the same time be more subtle about how you communicate the Halal and religious aspects in your branding, promotional activities, and locations - or vice versa.

From this, you'll start getting a sense that I do not believe in a one-size-fits-all approach to Halal Branding. This is about a path of discovery to establish what strategic branding approach will help you to achieve your aims and objectives. This means that you have to work on creating your own rich blend and recipe, which takes time and iterations.

So, having made these points, I'd like to bring this overview to an end and get on with the task at hand.

Read on...

02

UNDERSTANDING THE HALAL PHENOMENON

CHAPTER TWO:

UNDERSTANDING THE HALAL PHENOMENON

Islam is a belief system linked to civilisations with rich and transformational traditions: and its presence in Muslim lifestyle choices, business and commerce appears to be on the rise – spearheaded by Halal.

At the 9th World Islamic Economic Forum (WIEF) in 2013, I saw Malaysian Prime Minister H.E. Dato' Sri Mohd Najib Tun Abdul Razak, recount the story of Khadijah, the first convert to Islam.

"Of all the merchants in Mecca, she was the most successful; an entrepreneur who managed an international trading empire. One day, she hired a young man by the name of Muhammad, who she would eventually marry."

This was the same Muhammad who at the age of 25 married a 40 year old Khadijah; and then later as a 40 year old man received a revelation from the angel Gabriel, thus anointing him as the Prophet of Islam. This story serves as a further reminder of the cultural importance and opportunity to integrate business within the Muslim faithful's lifestyle, and it is where my discussions begin.

There are clear indications that the Halal industry has moved from niche to mainstream, and beyond its initial remit - which I have termed previously as 'meat and money' (Halal meat and Islamic finance). Halal as a concept, certification process, and lifestyle choice now underpins practices and consumption in: all food and drink, fashion, cosmetics, pharmaceuticals and healthcare, tourism and hospitality, marriage services, arts and entertainment, professional services, digital, and education. It's also likely to grow further into areas such as sports, leather goods and upholstery, and research ethics.

This chapter is not meant to be your guide on how to certify products. Rather, it is designed to give you a practical working knowledge of Islam in a business context, why Halal within this context is a cultural phenomenon, and how the various sectors embracing Halal may influence its practices today and in the future.

ORIGINS OF HALAL

Halal is an Arabic word linked to the Islamic faith. Halal in its general sense can be translated as meaning allowed, or permissible. A basic acceptance and understanding of what is Halal, is central to every Muslim's belief - falling under the umbrella of what is considered to be information that is known by necessity.

The opposite of this word in Arabic is Haram . A general rule of Islamic jurisprudence holds everything as Halal, unless stated otherwise.

Therefore a Muslim (follower of Islam) who has a sound

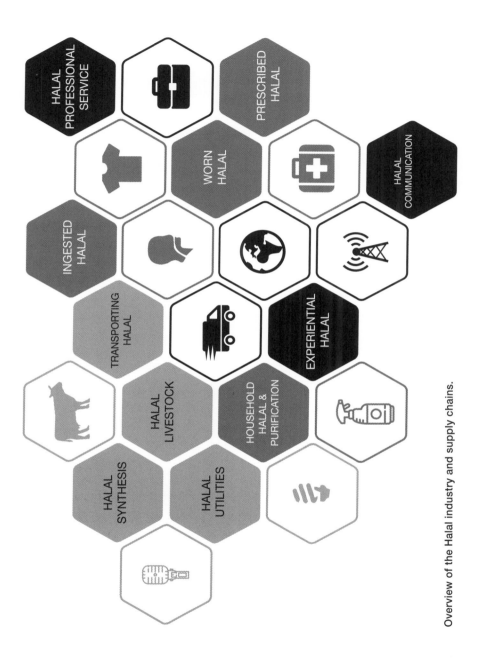

Overview of the Halal industry and supply chains.

grounding in Islam, should be able to identify what is Halal and what is not.

In contrast, Haram appears to resonate in the eyes of individuals with much stronger sentiments. This is because the conscious consumption of or engagement in haram activities, without repentance, carries with them the risk of spiritual or physical punishments (in the hereafter, or within Islamic law, respectively). As a result Muslims tend to adopt a position of avoidance, in the face of doubt.

WHAT DOES HALAL MEAN TODAY?

The call to certify products, services, and practices formally, and subsequently then label, logo, and brand them 'Halal' has given rise to what can be viewed as a new cultural phenomenon. No other religious or non-religious community or ideology is attempting to frame, regulate, and control decisions, choices, and activities in the same way, on such a large scale – across cultures and geographies.

If we look to pluralist Muslim nations like Malaysia today, in the context of food the term non-Halal is used in preference to Haram, in the signage of non-Muslim restaurants. This appears to confirm the perceptions of the word haram encouraging censure, by both Muslims and non-Muslims, and the desire for wider cultural sensitivity.

Interestingly, the appetite from Muslims and non-Muslims for Halal activities and opportunities are now also widespread in non-Muslim countries. So much so, that these inter-linked clusters of industry sectors have been valued at several trillion US dollars and growing. They are no longer just a religious imperative driven by Muslim clergy and the Muslim faithful: businesses play a crucial role in facilitating Muslims' ability to celebrate lifestyle choices, express their faith-based identities, and share their rich heritage.

In the following models, I've sought to show the various industry sectors as being linked, and also essentially grouped into three categories:

1. Utilities
2. Items of consumption (ingested and worn), and purification
3. Services and Experiences

Furthermore, Halal has championed an increased desire in many consumers, regardless of their faith, to be reassured of transparent and secure processes of manufacture and service delivery, which they seek to check.

The next phase of development has been the new wave of Muslim bloggers and entrepreneurs, spearheaded largely by women, who have crossed over into the mainstream - notably in the fashion, cosmetics, and food sectors.

Key drivers motivating them have been desires to share the human element and stories supporting these activities, which are so essential; alongside a striving in reaction to 9/11, terrorism, and some negative perceptions and fear of Muslims – both as mechanisms for building bridges, overcoming stereotypes, and generating greater economic stability and job opportunities.

THE GROWING MUSLIM CARAVAN OF INFLUENCE

One quarter of the world's population is Muslim, with well over half of Muslims today under the age of 25. Furthermore, the number of Muslims is expected to increase by over 35% in the next 20 years.

When considering the acronyms for the emerging economies to watch: in 2001 it was BRIC (Brazil, Russia, India, and China); and more recently in 2013 MINT (Mexico, Indonesia, Nigeria, Turkey), and CIVETS (Columbia, Indonesia, Vietnam, Egypt, Turkey and South Africa) – then it is apparent that economies with large Muslim populations are growing in importance.

I believe that we have now reached a tipping-point; where over the past decade there has been a marked interest and renewed openness towards addressing Muslim issues in business. This is a due to the following factors:

- The significance of wealth and resources within Muslim nations
- International trade agreements
- Economic migrancy
- Visibility in popular culture and the media
- The number of conversions to Islam outside of the Muslim world
- Population projections highlighting a young and growing Muslim population
- Recognition of a global, yet at the same time nuanced and local, transnational community; who are bound together and unified as a segment when targeted in a way that propagates Islamic values
- Increased cross-border information exchanges afforded by social media
- The democratisation of information, which affords consumers increased power, legitimacy and urgency
- Financial crises, economic recession, and debates on corporate and social responsibility; which have driven people towards further soul-searching and the quest for alternative economic systems, and guiding principles
- The continued affirmation from Muslim communities

that an Islamic identity defines who they are, how they live, and their terms of engagement.

Three arguments are usually presented to justify the imperative for operationalizing Islam-centric business models, which are as follows:

1. Economic argument:

Which relies on deductive findings, based upon data that is presented to demonstrate the market potential through financial value, geographies, and future sustainability through growing population figures.

2. Consumer-based perspective:

Which posits that beyond market value and size, there exists a consumer-based religious obligation to develop the sector, also inherent in their faith. There are growing needs and wants, with desires to align these with Islam and varying Muslim identities, regardless of temporal gains.

3. Geopolitical imperative:

Where commerce linked with Islam is influenced by geopolitics, and is held to be crucial when building international relations, political stability, and unique, yet collaborative and co-dependent national brand equities.

MUSLIM INFLUENCE

 One quarter of the world's population is Muslim

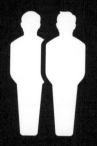 Over half of Muslims today are under the age of 25

 The number of Muslims is expected to increase by over 35% in the next 20 years

However, these perhaps are not reflective enough of the true nature of Halal, or embody the full range of its potential critical success factors. Furthermore, it is questionable whether we are witnessing developments in Islamic markets (as is often posited) or Muslim, or even culturally/ethnically centric markets.

Pragmatically, it could be argued that what we have are Muslim markets and economies, with the aspiration of creating an Islamic system, through the sum total of Muslim economies galvanizing themselves under a banner of 'Brand Islam'. Or alternatively, this may be about Muslim geographies and ethnic groups, drawing from Islamic frames of reference and schools of thought collaboratively.

On first reading, these two perspectives may appear to be saying the same thing. However, the order in which this process happens will yield differing consequences. The first is a bottom-up approach, and the second top-down.

WHY HALAL IS A NEW CULTURAL PHENOMENON

It would be easy to dismiss this simply as being the commercialisation and commodification of religion by industry, however there are strong indications that this is being driven also by consumers.

There are two key influencing factors that are encouraging consumer engagement:

9/11 and Islamist labelled terrorism:

Firstly, we are seeing Muslims searching for a way to reach out and harness the sprit of spirituality in a post 9/11 era - in an attempt to re-claim their religion and challenge wider negative perceptions.

Similar patterns of behaviour can be found historically, following social and geopolitical events affecting post-war Germany, Japan, and the African-American civil rights movement.

Parallels can also be drawn with sentiments expressed during the Industrial Revolution, which are largely attributed to Christian entrepreneurs: of wealth and value creation being moral acts – and acts of worship intended to pave the roads of paradise for the faithful on earth and in the hereafter.

The sentiments are very much that:

- Religion does have a place in business - offering an additional or revised set of guiding principles and moral compass
- Religious beliefs are a key segmentation criterion and trait
- Business can be a vehicle for transformational social change linked to religion
- An Islamic or Muslim economy offers a new unit of analysis in addition to national and geographical ones - which redefines boundaries and tends towards a more cultural and fluid frame of reference
- Islamic or Halal economics is a contemporary and grounded approach - attempting to challenging some counterproductive current worldviews of Islam, which often pose Islam as being a construct that is de-coupled from the West, or Capitalism - through focusing on social interaction and transactions in the widest sense.

A Social Media Flat Earth:

Secondly, social media is flattening and fattening the earth. It affords consumers the ability to engage with each other across geographies - and with social, economic and business issues much more than before.

This has expanded the net of stakeholder engagement further away from narrow-based perspectives of stakeholders being defined as people upon whom a business relies upon for survival, towards broad-based views where a stakeholder is someone who has an interest and a voice.

More so than ever, consumers have a voice on various platforms, which gift them self-defined Power, Legitimacy, and Urgency. Furthermore, there has been a democratisation of information that allows individuals and collectives the opportunity to debate, mediate, collaborate, create, and adjudicate.

I call this a type of collective individualism, which functions in a much more dynamic and consensual manner.

A clear case in practice can be seen by examining the Arab Spring – spearheaded through social media, operating as a leaderless opposition movement, where varied and differing interpretations were expressed by citizen activist groups.

Many opinions were formulated and consensus arrived at through social media discussions and desk/phone-based research, which drew from an eclectic blend of traditions;

SO MANY MEDIA
STORIES ANNOUNCE
GAZILLIONS AND
KATRILLIONS OF
MUSLIM DOLLARS -

**BUT HOW DO YOU
BENEFIT?**

tribalism; history; politics; economics; technology adoption; and contemporary, popular, and counter-culture.

CONTEMPORARY DEFINITIONS OF HALAL AND ISLAMIC MARKETING

Also, in connection with Halal and Islamic finance, currently there are debates that question what Islamic Marketing actually means. The argument offered being that these fields necessitate alternative Islamic and marketing approaches. For example, does it (Islamic marketing) only consider how marketers should communicate with Muslims - or whether being a Muslim is an essential element needed to execute Islamic marketing?

A fundamental development now is that the field is more than simply marketing a religion, or marketing to the faithful. Furthermore, John Grant and I argued in a paper published in the *Journal of Islamic Marketing*, if Islamic Marketing is posited as a subset of religion, then it runs the risk of being a fad. If mainstream marketing is superior in its theory base, effectiveness, and ability now to embrace aspects of Islam, then Islamic Marketing as a field or term becomes redundant. Or, if Islamic Marketing does not present a set of theories, concepts and approaches that are sufficiently different, then again it offers little.

If Halal, Islamic Finance and Marketing are to cement their legitimacy and unique attributes over the long term, then these factors have to be considered. Also, like other niche areas that have crossed over to being viewed as mass transnational markets, these constructs have to evolve.

Just as the Chinese have brought us new terms and concepts such as *guanxi* (social relations) and *mianzi* (maintaining one's face); and likewise the Japanese with *kaizen* (improvement and change for the best) and *kanban* (just-in-time production): the modern Muslim world has to work on defining, explaining, applying, and marketing specific characteristics.

In light of these observations, I came up with the following working definition of Islamic Marketing, of which Branding is a component - that sees it existing on three interdependent levels:

1. The acknowledgement of a God-conscious approach to Marketing: from a marketer's and/or consumer's perspective, which draws from the drivers or traits associated with Islam

2. A progressive and contemporary school of thought, which has a moral compass that tends towards the ethical norms and values of Islam and how Muslims interpret these today, from their varying cultural lenses

3. A multi-layered, dynamic and contextual gestalt phenomenon of Muslim and non-Muslim stakeholder engagement, which considers the creation and preservation of explicit, implicit and tacit signalling associated with Islam. These cues, triggers and networks are embodied by objects and experiences - which give rise to reciprocal cultural artefacts, that are facilitated by Marketing.

Therefore, my suggestion here is that the bedrock of marketing products and services successfully should rely upon an approach that is predominantly ethnocentric, which I outline in a subsequent model.

Whilst ethnocentrism is often perceived as being a negative trait: for me, it is an unavoidable reality of human experiences, reinforced by established flourishing networks. In reality, communities, consciously or unconsciously, hold their culture to be of more significance than others, and therefore champion it – with positive or negative effects.

You might wonder why in these definitions I have avoided using the term Sharia. This is because the term Sharia law is often misunderstood, met with trepidation by some, and perhaps fails to communicate what the Sharia is, and is designed for.

HALAL MARKETING IS MORE ABOUT
ETHNICITY & CULTURE

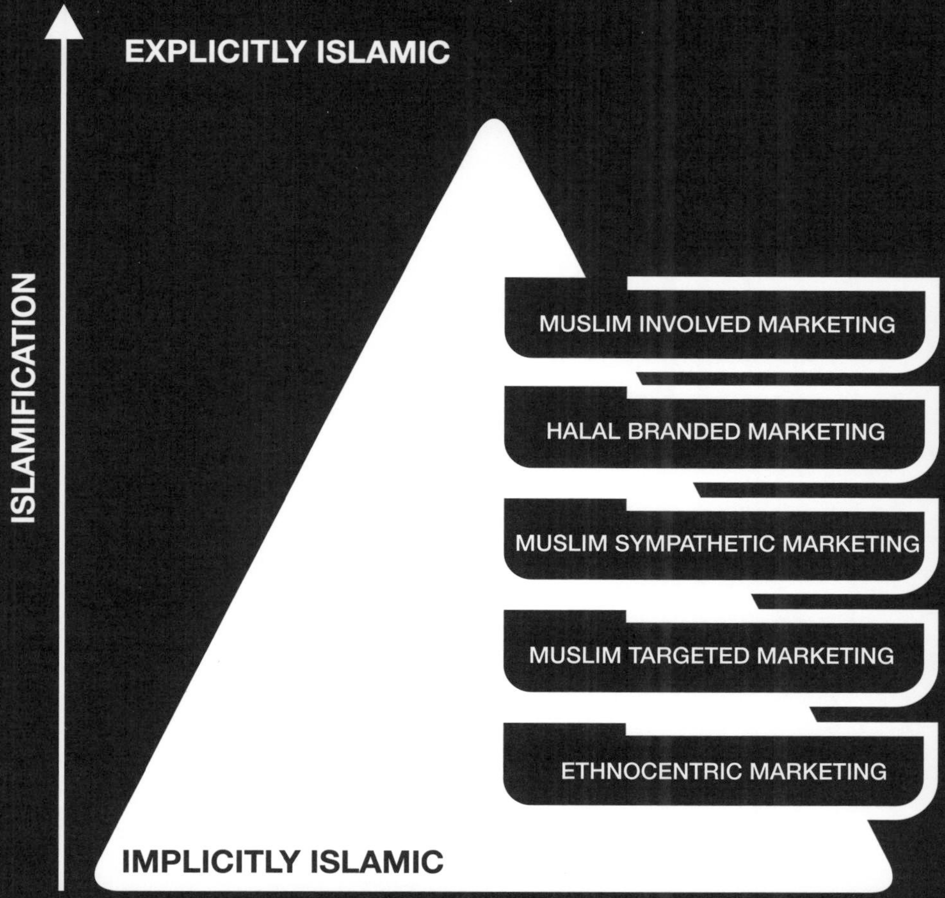

EXPLICITLY ISLAMIC

ISLAMIFICATION

MUSLIM INVOLVED MARKETING

HALAL BRANDED MARKETING

MUSLIM SYMPATHETIC MARKETING

MUSLIM TARGETED MARKETING

ETHNOCENTRIC MARKETING

IMPLICITLY ISLAMIC

A more correct translation of the Arabic word Sharia is 'well trodden path' - as it is has a wider remit, covering crime, politics, economics, business, science, family relations, hygiene, diet, moral conduct, etiquette, and worship.

Marketers and Halal certification bodies often highlight Sharia compliance and target predominantly those partners and consumers who seek compliance - rendering the product offering as niche and a rationally-based consumption item, which does not necessarily encompass the emotional and lifestyle elements linked to cultural tradition.

Instead, my argument presented in the model is that moving up or down the pyramid equally can be strategic corporate objectives. However, also there is no reason why the same objectives could not be attempted in tan-

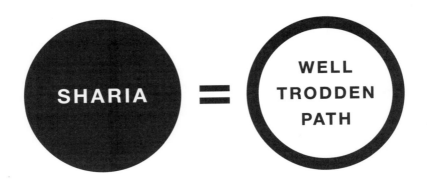

dem, instead of in a sequential hierarchy.

Following the same train of thought, all Marketing Communications should contain a depth of encoded messages that appeal to defined selections of homogenous segments. Furthermore, shared culture and ethnocentrism are held to be unifying factors that can mediate heterogeneity. These are all aspects that I will explore in more detail in Chapter Five.

THE CHALLENGE OF MASS-PRODUCTION AND GLOBALISATION

In the initial stages of Halal development, it could be argued that the reasons for its inception were that it was a reaction in Muslim minority or narrow majority populations for a need to provide assurances that food was fit for Muslim consumption and it presented an opportunity for Muslim economic and business growth.

Therefore, we can view these in two phases. The first being where Muslims took their inspiration from the Jewish community in the USA - by checking and overtly labeling their food. Following this, there was the realization that 'Halal' could offer economic stability in terms of consumption and commerce, and move the balance of power in favor of the Muslim community.

Growing consumer demand and market opportunities mean that there has never been a point in history before where so many people across the globe are requesting or being served Halal items.

I heard from Emirates Airlines for example that they serve approximately 125,000 Halal meals a day on their airplanes. Non-Muslim nations like New Zealand and Australia have moved to a position where the majority of their red meat production is Halal slaughtered and certified. Also, I have heard first hand from Halal certifiers that abattoirs in Brazil are producing and exporting anywhere up to 1,500 Halal chickens per plant, per day. But it's worth noting that this is still half the number of non-Halal chickens per day from similar sized Brazilian plants.

However, many non-Muslim nations are worried about being too overt in their fandom, for fear of being labelled religious fanatic lovers, by a vocal minority of anti-Muslim sentiment. Some of the key non-Muslim countries that I'd like to single out as supporting the Halal economy are: Australia, Brazil, China, Italy, Japan, New Zealand, South Korea, Spain, Thailand, United Kingdom, and United States of America.

At a corporate level, there are two types of business who are shaping the Halal space:

- **For-Muslim markets businesses** - where a portion of their business exists in the Halal ecosystem, and who see halal as an enabler and linked to a form of ethnic or localized marketing
- **Born Halal ready businesses** – largely owned by Muslims, who live, breathe, and think Halal, because it's the way they want to live their lives and do business.

Within these classifications, businesses are well aware of the potential, but many haven't quite worked out how to do good halal branding, or aren't sufficiently able to invest time and resources into finding out and producing world beating brands.

To further complicate matters, we have to look forward to the changing sands of Halal standards and certification. This is a very complicated area, and very much work in progress - where we're having to update thinking, innovate in a positive and authentically Islamic way; and that means bringing together thought from fiqh (interpretation of Islamic law), madhabs (schools of thought within fiqh), business

and management, marketing, behavioural psychology, sociology, agriculture and food sciences.

For example, one of the areas that I have identified is the use of genetically modified crops that are insect resistant. On the face of it, it makes perfect sense to maximize the harvest of usable crops, and to avoid using pesticides. However, from my own Islamic perspective I wonder whether Muslims should create 'pest' resistant plants that effectively will bring the extinction of certain insects, which are also creation of Allah and must have been created for a reason, and with his wisdom.

Also, Halal Logistics and Supply Chains have become growing areas of concern and interest, with the realisation that meat storage and transportation is open to contamination risks, which, not to mention, also may effect previously unconsidered food items like biscuits, that may have moved on a factory conveyor belt lubricated by pork-based lubricants.

In response, at the other end of the spectrum, there are independent organic Muslim owned farms that are delivering locally sourced bespoke organic chickens on demand for approximately £17 GBP per chicken.

SHOULD MUSLIMS CREATE 'PEST' RESISTANT PLANTS THAT EFFECTIVELY WILL BRING THE EXTINCTION OF CERTAIN INSECTS?

Following these points, I believe that ethics also have to play a pivotal role. I take my evidence from the following:

"Allah's Messenger (Prophet Muhammad) cursed ten people in connection with (alcoholic) wine: the wine-presser, the one who has it pressed, the one who drinks it, the one who conveys it, the one to whom it is conveyed, the one who serves it, the one who sells it, the one who benefits from the price paid for it, the one who buys it, and the one for whom it is bought."

(Hadith related by Al-Tirmidhi).

Whilst the drinking of alcohol for recreational purposes is prohibited in Islam, this hadith also demonstrates that the involvement in, encouragement and consumption of this commodity is also forbidden.

Therefore I argue for the decommoditisation of Halal concepts, in favour of treating them as processes - where the behaviour and intentions of those involved also fall under scrutiny.

This would push practices towards approaches such as: Fair Trade, corporate altruism, sustainability and green marketing. In doing so however, further consideration would have to be made as to which products and services would credibly still remain within this reworked Halal framework.

Products that profess such levels of ethical practice tend to position themselves as carrying a premium. In contrast, many current Halal offerings adopt strategies that price them below their non-Halal equivalents, if not cheaper. This is to encourage their consumption - either for religious or commercial reasons (and in some cases both).

Therefore, my suggestion is that Halal supply chain optimization will encounter difficulties, when addressing management issues surrounding brand value fully. This is due to the fact that conventional definitions of better quality products, delivered more quickly, for lower costs, and with a stronger brand presence, do not constitute what is considered Halal – according to definitions derived from Islam.

Illustrating this, the following two hadith and a chapter in the Qur'an form the cornerstone of Islamic judgements:

"All actions are judged by intention"

(First phrase extract from a hadith related by Al-Bukhari and Muslim, as a reported saying of the prophet Muhammad)

"Whoever commits an act, or introduces a matter into our

religion (Islam), which is not part of it, will have it rejected"

(Hadith related by Al-Bukhari and Muslim, as a reported saying of the prophet Muhammad)

"I (Allah) swear by time, that I have created, that all of mankind is at loss; except for those that (do all of the following): believe (in Islam), do good deeds, guide people to truth and have patience"

(Qur'an, chapter 103)

[Translation by the author, from the texts, in Arabic]

Most likely, from a consumer's perspective, the drivers for actively selecting Halal are governed by people who:

- Are consciously Muslim (influenced by religiosity)
- Are consciously Muslim (influenced by a cultural identity)
- Identify with the concept of monotheism across the Abrahamic faiths (Judaism, Christianity, and Islam)
- See Halal as a form of societal inclusivity and relationship building
- See Halal as a necessary ingredient in order to ensure Muslim participation
- View it as a welcome extra layer of scrutiny.

These form the basis for initiating rationally and emotionally-based intentions.

Only once these have been achieved, can a review of the supply chain process occur, with its subsequent optimization.

Faced with the challenges of growth: organizations need to focus on heritage, provenance, legitimacy, fair treatment of workers, and being more able to implement a hands-on approach to celebrating Islamic values on how Halal is being marketed and branded throughout the supply chain.

However, also they need to have an eye on processes too: industrialization and automation are key growth factors when delivering at scale – and so a key consideration lies in dictating how far to go down these routes. This is the difficult and proactive middle-path that Muslims strive for.

Therefore, Halal has to become the global vanguard for defending ethical and moral principles, traceability, and sustainability, and that has to be for the entire economic pyramid - not just for white collar, affluent middle class Muslims as a lifestyle choice.

Halal could be the vehicle by which consumers, using their smart phones could check the entire supply chain, and assess the Halal credentials, right down to the farm, oceans, date of harvest, corporate and social responsibilities, restaurant, everything… because if you think about it, you could have Halal farmed and slaughtered meat, but how do you know that it's been transported, stored, and prepared in a halal way?

THE CASE FOR HALAL AS A BRAND, OR A BRAND ETHOS?

If the nature of Halal exists within product and brand theory, a question arises whether Halal can successfully be defined as forming a commercial commodity, a brand, or a combination of both?

I believe that Halal as a concept cannot be fully encapsulated only within these constructs. Instead it is a philosophy, which whilst apparent and effective in branding, marketing and product development, stretches much further into disciplines such as management, organizational behaviour, cultural anthropology, sociology and spirituality.

Halal's roots pre-date formalized marketing and branding practices, therefore in attempting to house it within these constructs, it is akin to attempting to contain the oceans. Instead marketing and brand thinking has to adapt in order to accommodate and preserve the essence of what Halal actually is.

If Halal is treated as a brand, there is unlikely to be a case where the name Halal could be adopted outright. Therefore its usage would suggest one that positions it as an ingredient brand or compound word, almost assuming the role of a co-brand. For example, Halal-OtherWord, or OtherWord-Halal. As a co-brand, a global organization could create a corporate division, which utilizes the term Halal.

POSSIBLE NEW WAYS OF
NAMING AND LABELLING

Following this, emerging future practices may yield names such as: Nestlé Halal, Innocent Halal, British Airways Halal, or Cobra Zero Halal beer. However, this would bring more of an organization's practices under further scrutiny - for example the treatment of employees and their associated working environment. This is because service providers' food would have to comply with Halal specifications and more efforts would have to be made to preserve Islamic rituals, such as Ramadan and prayer .

Whilst this may appear to be a bold step, it could in fact be an effective strategy when entering Muslim markets – by reducing mistrust and consumer distance, due to what are often perceived as being confusing and somewhat schizophrenic corporate practices.

Through this ring-fencing, organizations can distil their strategies, removing the potential for over-kill – as individually branding each product offering with Halal, will reduce the term's efficacy.

Such approaches would be a departure though from basic Islamic principles - where everything is Halal, unless stated otherwise. However, they may serve as cues - encouraging and reassuring stakeholders of their Halal legitimacy.

HALAL BRANDING AS AN OFFENSIVE AND/OR DEFENSIVE CORPORATE STRATEGY

The Halal market has seen a growing number of products outside of the food sector, overtly carrying Islamic classifications. Examples range from Halal soap, Halal perfume, Halal chocolate and even Islamic Hip-Hop.

Traditionally seen as being non-contentious commodities, explanations for this phenomenon can be viewed in two ways: Optimistically, they serve as a positive reinforcement of the demand for such commodities and their economic market potential. However a polemical case can be argued for increased concerns driving such growth, within the Muslim community.

Muslims may feel that not enough of their needs are being catered for, perhaps there remains a mistrust of larger organizations, or feelings of a lack of control over the Islamic standard.

In support of this pessimism, there are cases where minute trace elements of alcohol or haram animal products have been found in commodities - despite carrying labeling indicating otherwise. This shows that whilst not considered significant within general manufacturing practices, they are still areas of concern for Muslims.

In a quest for Islamic purity, Muslims believe that the purification of faith, understanding, wealth, and actions lead to levels of greater spirituality.

These sentiments provide admirable aspirations and great potential, for marketers and brands - whereby consumers sees themselves as being one with the product or service in question, by collectively and if possible collaboratively, achieving Halal credentials.

SUMMARY AND THE ROAD AHEAD

Muslims continue to grab headlines, regarding their religious beliefs, practices, political views, role in society and of course geopolitical events.

On the other hand, whilst globalisation and transnationalism appears to be steering mainstream business thought and practice on a path towards apoliticism for fear of a backlash, Muslim majorities and minorities are raising the flag for the importance and role of guiding principles derived from religion - which as a result of the current landscape has also rendered it infused with politics and ideological struggle.

In postmodern, capitalist, and secular societies: overtly discussing and celebrating religion in business, and especially Islam, is considered to be taboo. However, Muslim thought is signalling strongly that a code of ethics has to permeate business practice in such a way that business is a collective and societal obligation; and that wider stakeholders outside of organisations are empowered to hold businesses to account - according to legal principles, which encompass the wider facets of human existence.

In this vein, Halal is inextricably linked to Muslim life - and the recent Halal phenomenon is a case in practice of Muslim and Islamic thought progressing to keep in step with the modern world and globalisation.

In addition it is evidence of how the Sharia can evolve and adapt, according to time and context. Furthermore, it highlights the indelible significance of religion within the Muslim psyche, when both consuming and conducting business. Unfortunately, media coverage is split in reporting whether Halal's visible increase, or by extension, indicators of proposed sense of religiosity, is a good thing or not.

By way of an analogy, if Islam was viewed as an organisation: the assumption is that it has legitimacy - and organisational theory dictates that performance is clearly very much dependent on the perceptions and practices of internal and external stakeholders.

Therefore from this perspective, there needs to be a greater focus on how Islam is interpreted and enacted inside and outside of the religion, rather than debunking Islam per se.

In addition, with Islamic perspectives featuring more and

more in business practices and academia, I believe that transformational solutions with wider implications will arise from business schools and industry.

In the case of Muslims and Halal: on one level concerns are rooted in geopolitics, societal issues, and culture - for which Islam is carrying the can or flag, depending on your standpoint.

However my view, going back to the organisation analogy, is that more accurately, the rate-determining step is about managing issues of scalability, rather than theology.

Muslims and non-Muslims are concerned with understanding, mediating, and managing the scale of a Halal lifestyle, in an increasingly connected and global theatre.

If I paint a utopian picture of a small and effectively gated countryside community of monotheists, with free access to resources, equal social standing and rights: then fewer individuals would have problems with establishing links of trade and commerce, free-exchanges, or forging friendships across groups.

However, the reality is that with increased interconnectivity, and a greater and wider number of influencing factors: a cultural osmosis is occurring on levels where the stakes are much higher; and actors are in pursuit of greater levels of power and asymmetry.

HALAL UTILITIES

Energy & Water

HALAL LIVESTOCK

Animal Transportation & Cargo

Slaughter

Animal Testing

HALAL SYNTHESIS

Drugs, Chemicals & Polymers

Cleaners & Detergents

TRANSPORTING HALAL

Business Transport

Logistics Carbon Footprint

Halal Containers

Cleansing Services

Livestock & Animal Cargo

Postal and Courier

INGESTED HALAL

Crops & Agriculture

Non-alcoholic Drinks & Beverages

Meat & Poultry Products

Food Products

Genetically Modified Food & Substance

Supplements

WORN HALAL

Toiletries & Cosmetics

Wearing Apparel

Sythetic & Animal Fabrics

Leather Goods

HOUSEHOLD HALAL & PURIFICATION

Cleaners & Detergents

Gardening & Horticulture

Pets & Petcare

Synthetic & Animal Fabrics

Leather Goods

PRESCRIBED HALAL

Pharmatecual & Healthcare
- Drugs
- Implants
- Medical Services

Medical Tourism

Spiritual Tourism

HALAL PROFESSIONAL SERVICE

Certification

Employment & Human Resource Managment

Organisational Behaviour, Legal, Accounting & Professional Services

Financial Services
- Bank & Building Societies
- Loans, Credit Cards & Mortgages
- Insurance
- Investments & Bonds
- Online Transactions

Government & Non-profit Organisations

Education & Training

EXPERIENTIAL HALAL

Restaurants

Events, Hospitality & Hotels

Leisure, Entertainment & Games

Creative Arts

Consumer Travel, Transport & Tourism
- General Transport
- Holidays
- Medical Tourism
- Spiritual Tourism

Property & Construction of Halal Spaces

Halal Retail Spaces

Online & Virtual Communities

HALAL COMMUNICATION CHANNELS

Media & Publishing

Advertising, Branding & Public Relations

Web 2.0, Social Media, Citizen Journalism & User Generated Content

Matrimonial Services & Websites

Figure: Grouping Halal industries according to commodities and consumption

Just as with other macro issues such as megacities, Islam is now in the spotlight and Muslims are being asked questions about the scale of their presence and practices. These issues in my view can only be addressed through continued open dialogue, open mindedness, good spiritedness, and trial and error.

I do concede that this roadmap is not easy, when still under a shadow of 9/11, and a series of other historical and continuing events – all of which are encouraging parties to adopt protectionist, ossified and binary polar positions.

The spirit of spirituality, and profiting from the legacy of Prophethood are the sliver lining to shadows cast by the 9/11 cloud. A balance of transient and transcendent ethics are central to all of this - but work still needs to be done, where enough processes and principles are articulated to businesses or consumers clearly, and to a level that is expected in the world today.

03

MARKETS & CONSUMPTION PATTERNS

CHAPTER THREE:

MARKETS AND CONSUMPTION PATTERNS

ISLAMIC LEGACY AND REALITY

Islam as a way of life, a philosophy, a religion, and a belief system, rooted in culture, is both evolutionary and revolutionary. This means that it balances liberalist and conservative standpoints, which often leads to differences in opinion.

For example, some consumers prefer tribal systems and hierarchies, where individual decision-making is sacrificed for the greater good and consensus within a community. However, especially with younger consumers, consumption, religious views and opinions are decided through consensus using social media and the gathering of a wide range of Internet based information – as a form of *collective individualism.*

One thing that can be observed is that historically, Islam has always driven urbanisation and this has been taken forward by urbanites, who seek to maintain a link with nature and spread knowledge. Therefore, in present day society, especially with the significance of the Internet and city life, Islam is well placed to embrace global developments. Just as city life and Internet consumption have to mediate conservative and more liberal standpoints, this is not a new reality for the Muslim community – as historically the Muslim civilization and Silk Route joined vast landmasses. However, what still needs to be addressed and updated today is how Muslims define and assert their own perspectives, with the rise of other civilizations and ideologies.

HALAL BRANDING AS A MEANS OF REDUCING MUSLIM CONSUMER DISSONANCE

Within Muslim countries and especially those which have Arabic as their mother tongue, many products have previously taken their Halal status as a given. However, many offerings now seek to brand themselves as Halal - even within Arab speaking and Muslim nations. This is especially in cases where products are viewed as being foreign, or potentially contentious.

For example it may be more crucial to brand *Han* originating Chinese food (largely hailing from a non-Muslim majority) as Halal, in comparison to popular dishes native to Chinese Muslim tribes and Muslim countries.

Due to the concept of avoidance of doubt, Halal branding is in some way differentiated from other ingredient brands, such as 'Fair Trade' or 'sugar free' and is more comparable to: 'sugar free'(for diabetics), 'suitable for vegetarians', or 'nut free' - where consumers have indelible laws of guidance.

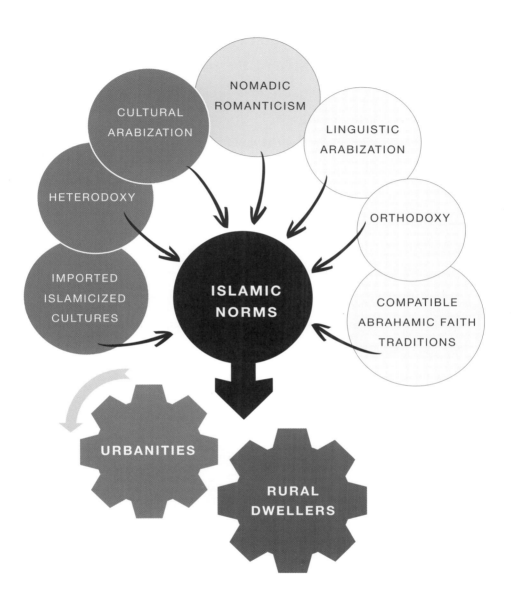

BALANCING REVOLUTIONARY HETERODOXY WITH CONSERVATIVE ORTHODOXY

CHANGING HALAL CONSUMPTION PATTERNS

Therefore, another reason for the Halal phenomenon continuing to gain traction, in a similar way to organic, fair trade, and other initiatives, is driven by the need to identify, regulate, control, track, and communicate far more processes and activities.

This is expanding the remit and definition of Halal in such a way that it is encapsulating more of the classical interpretations as to what Halal is and is for – where mere permissibility is no longer enough. Now, consumers are becoming more interested in quality, wholesomeness [*tayyib* in Arabic], provenance, corporate ethical principles and social responsibility.

Being a Muslim is not necessarily a defining factor as to whether these propositions are appealing to businesses or consumers. This is very much about mind-sharing, and developing an alternative business model and value proposition, which crosses over. Niche is becoming mainstream.

This is especially the case when Muslim and non-Muslim business owners offer their products and services to everyone, driven by a desire to cater for as many people as possible. In the case of Muslim business owners, it's also an expression of authentic values, which they hold and wish to share as a form of worship with integrity.

Secondly, as I mentioned earlier, the majority view is that Halal is the norm and Haram, or non-Halal, is the exception. Whilst I concur with this construct as a general principle, it appears that the recent phenomenon of creating Halal logos and branding strategies have created both opportunities and challenges, which are changing classical interpretations and understanding of what Halal is.

The drivers for this are a type of hyper-sensitivity and hyper-interactivity which are encouraged by:

- The commodification of entities through branding and national boundary ownership
- Hyper-information exchanges and education, which bring constituent components under scrutiny
- The mass-manufacture of bulk commodities
- Technological and genetic engineering advancements
- Challenges by single issue politics and anti-branding movements

This is especially interesting, as the phenomenon of branding products as Halal is also being practiced in countries, such as the Kingdom of Saudi Arabia, with almost exclusive Muslim majorities.

Whilst some may see this as a positive movement encouraging Muslim commerce and consumption, underpinned by Islam, it is also possible that a by-product may be the repositioning of Halal labelling as a hygiene factor.

A hygiene factor is a concept, which argues that the absence of this element (such as a Halal logo) leads to dissatisfaction, and could encourage greater perceived consumer risk and suspicion. There is a real risk also that it may make Muslims more risk averse by nature, and this could impact on their ability to push the boundaries of innovation and creativity.

HALAL BRANDING AS A TOOL FOR PROMOTING FAITH – *BRAND ISLAM*

By taking an alternative interpretation of the avoidance of doubt concept, a case can still be made for Halal possessing similar attributes to conscious consumption and ethical ingredient brands, in that consumers are likely to want to support such products or services, because:

- There are fears that a lack of commercial success will drive producers away from producing Halal products and services
- There will be associated commercial benefits for Muslims
- This is seen as a form of Islamic worship and assertion of Islamic identity
- This is viewed by Muslims as a legitimate form of Is-

lamic proselytization - which will encourage a climate of Islamic acceptance. Muslims inviting people to Islam, known as *da'wah* in Arabic, is seen as being central to their beliefs and a praiseworthy act. Whilst sometimes this has been profiled as having sinister undertones - in contrast by the vast majority of Muslims, it is simply an enactment of the hadith and saying of the Prophet Muhammad (peace be upon him): *"None of you truly has faith, until you love for your brothers and sisters, that which you love for yourself"*.

IS MUSLIM LOYALTY FORMED IN A DIFFERENT WAY?
Beyond obvious conclusions which can be drawn, that Muslim loyalty is formed in a way where Islam is of more importance than in comparison with other non-Muslim segments, this may not translate into brand preference for Muslim brands. Furthermore, in markets where there are several Muslim brands, other factors may become more important.

Taste, tradition, tribalism, culture, national identity and nation branding appear to remain important variables not only for Muslims. Perhaps the surprising fact is that whilst Muslims profess to be part of one *ummah*, culture and national traits may in fact still be more important in the Muslim world than acknowledged.

Therefore in response, it makes better brand sense to treat Islam as a cultural construct and something that is fused with collective and individual interpretations of national identity – as nations have become a globally recognised unit of classification.

Muslim communities still centre around souk and barter cultures - so greater loyalty can be elicited through: customisations, varying and elastic sensitive pricing, customer intimacy, and overtly rewarding loyalty.

The challenge in modern markets and with the transparency afforded by the Internet and social media, is that responsive collaborative pricing may be difficult to maintain and execute, without unnecessarily eroding price margins. A way of protecting barter pricing and profits is to invest in the brand and to structure pricing and incentives linked to customisation, or group discounts.

Because of these two factors – consumer ambassadorship and ownership of Islam, and barter cultures: it is likely that maintaining brand loyalty may pose greater problems than for other consumer segments.

Muslims have been seen to be loyal to mainstream brands, also spending more, however there is a paucity of Muslim brand case examples to be able to test whether it would be the same, greater or even worse for a Muslim brand.

This is due to the fact that brands, which signal their affiliation with Islam, enjoy a duality of existence – where they are welcomed more, but also scrutinised more. That's one rule for Muslims and another rule for others.

DO MUSLIMS CHOOSE BRANDS IN DIFFERENT WAY TO NON-MUSLIMS?

The significance of culture

On one level, I argue that Muslims choose brands largely in the same way that other consumer segments do. This process can be explained as a human transactional equation.

$$HCE = ((IM) + (EM)) \xleftarrow{\textit{transactional}} \xrightarrow{\textit{exchange}} ((IT) + (ET))$$

HCE: Human Cultural Experience
IM: Internal Me
EM: External Me
IT: Internal Them
ET: External Them

Transactional exchange

Horizontal: free exchange, +ve outcomes
Horizontal: free exchange, -ve outcomes
Asymmetric: +ve (dominant), -ve (harmful)

Equation applied

Case One examples - simple

IM: Internal Me – I see myself as Chinese
EM: External Me – You see me as Chinese
IT: Internal Them – You see yourself as Chinese
ET: External Them – I see you as Chinese
Transactional exchange: Horizontal
Synergy, with +ve outcomes: **we understand each other and communication is productive**

IM: Internal Me - I see myself as Chinese
EM: External Me - You see me as Chinese
IT: Internal Them - You see yourself as Chinese
ET: External Them - I see you as Chinese
Transactional exchange: Horizontal
Disconnect, with -ve outcomes: **we understand each other and communication is counterproductive**

IM: Internal Me - I see myself as Chinese
EM: External Me - You see me as Chinese
IT: Internal Them - You see yourself as Chinese
ET: External Them - I see you as Chinese
Transactional exchange: +ve dominant
Synergy, with acceptance of one dominant view of Chinese culture over another

THE HUMAN TRANSACTIONAL EXCHANGE

HUMAN CULTURAL EXPERIENCE EQUATION =

[INTERNAL ME + EXTERNAL ME]	←→	[INTERNAL THEM + EXTERNAL THEM]
[HOW I SEE MYSELF + HOW I AM SEEN]	←→	[HOW THEY SEE THEMSELVES + HOW I SEE THEM]

TRANSACTIONAL EXCHANGE
Horizontal: free exchange, +ve outcomes
Horizontal: free exchange, -ve outcomes
Asymmetric: +ve (dominant), -ve (harmful)

IM: Internal Me - I see myself as Chinese
EM: External Me - You see me as Chinese
IT: Internal Them - You see yourself as Chinese
ET: External Them - I see you as Chinese
Transactional exchange: -ve dominant
Disconnect, with lack of acceptance of one dominant view of Chinese culture over another.

Case Two examples - intermediate

IM: Internal Me – I see myself as Chinese, English
EM: External Me – You see me as Chinese
IT: Internal Them – You see yourself as English
ET: External Them – I see you as English

IM: Internal Me – I see myself as Chinese, English
EM: External Me – You see me as Chinese
IT: Internal Them – You see yourself as a Londoner
ET: External Them – I see you as English
Again, there could be several types of transactional exchange, which have +ve or –ve outcomes.

Case Three examples – advanced

In most cases however, it's much more complicated and reflective of real human experiences that are dynamic, contextual, and time-specific (both transient and transcendent) – which if not understood, may frame humans as irrational, and capricious.

There needs to be a pull for branding strategists to capture and analyse data in real time – as it is this crucial, spontaneous, tacit and perishable knowledge that will dictate whether your brand can match the conscious and unconscious desires of your audience, and remain relevant.

Based upon Values, Attitudes and Behaviour, here are some examples of factors, which constitute collective human internal and external traits (non-exhaustive):

- Age
- Gender
- Income
- Cultural ethnicity
- Friendship bonds
- Family bonds
- Work bonds
- Size of networks
- Religion, faith and spirituality
- Places of travel
- Places of residence
- Acquired tastes
- Interests
- Level and area of education
- Languages

- Brands consumed
- Internet and technological literacy
- Rejected factors
- Trade-offs
- Frequency of purchase
- Recency of purchase
- Value of purchase
- Volume of purchase

Successful brands and businesses possess detailed data on all of these, and this therefore presents a big barrier for newer and growing businesses. Furthermore, if a business wants to collect this data, the challenges are whether:

- They can afford to do so
- They are equipped to be able to analyse, interpret and use this data
- Having done so, the data is still up-to date and relevant.

Also, each individual factor is not mutually exclusive – and so do not tend to represent a zero-sum game. Instead, building a body of knowledge and answers to these classifiers is cumulative - leading to wealth creation and is likely to yield further complicated hyphenated hybrid identities.

So for example, it is possible that someone can be

Chinese and English – but more importantly, that they can be 100% Chinese and/or 100% English, depending on the time and context.

This perspective supports the idea that individuals can be Global, whilst being locally(cultural)-centric. It also refutes the *Tebbit Test* argument that individuals make clear choices about a permanent national identity of being Chinese, or English, for example.

Furthermore, it challenges concepts of pluralism, multiculturalism and 'melting pots'. Instead, there is one cultural paradigm, with different levels, perspectives and interpretations – all of which are trying to deliver a shared human experience of existence.

To this end, cultural separation and differences, are merely means of problem solving, rather than an actual human reality. You have to look below the tip of the iceberg.

To conclude, this means that the challenge is in identifying what are the most dominant and influential factors. In doing so, it also presents various traits side by side.

So for example, for some people, religion may fulfil the function of being an ethnic identity, whilst for others it may be a moral compass, or even just an interest. Nevertheless, religion collectively presents itself as a common and reoccurring factor – which renders itself as something

ANGUAGES

ACES OF RESIDENCE   LANGUAGES

RELIGION,   INTEREST
FAITH AND
RITUALITY

REQUENCY OF PURCHASE   TECH
LITER

GENDER

AMILY BONDS   BRANDS CON

ACQUIRED   INCOME   INT
TASTES

INTERNET AM

IZE OF NETWORKS

CULTURAL   INC

ETHNICITY

DE-OFFS   LEVEL A
RED   GENDER   AREA
STES   RECENCY OF PURCHASE   EDUCATIO

Figure: Factors, which constitute collective human internal and external traits.

which defines and underpins humans, and their subsequent transactions and exchanges.

The implications are that, especially for future generations, without a refinement of traditional approaches and classifications of faith, which at times are monolithic, basic, or even insensitive: it will become increasingly difficult to track, place and understand individuals and collectives, where there are increasing choices.

I want to make my point clear here: the role of a branding and marketing professional is to first and foremost understand consumer behaviour through their eyes.

Secondarily, if you so wish, then you can consider arguments as to whether this aligns with your understanding of the faith. Finally then, you have the choice to decide how you wish to respond to consumer behaviours and demands.

Now I would like to give you some anecdotal examples of how terms, classifications and behavioural patterns can in fact be quite fluid. They are obvious, but nevertheless I like to remind myself of them to avoid my thinking becoming too rigid and surface-driven. For example:

- *Black People* is a term that means everything and nothing, depending on the context
- *Black Music* now is seen as being a genre, state of mind and self-defined affinity group term - rather than simply a

MARKETS & CONSUMPTION PATTERNS

means of identifying the race of the musician or audience

- Playing football for England or supporting the team no longer necessitates being born in England, or being white, Anglo-Saxon and Christian – even though the English flag is a cross, the symbol of Christianity
- Non-Japanese people may crave more authentic Japanese food than even some Japanese people
- You don't have to be employed by *Apple* in order to offer technical support
- Women can dress modestly, using layers of clothes, which individually are perhaps immodest or marketed in such a way, which conflicts with more modest dress codes and their values
- Conventionally 'bad students' could become 'great students', through using unconventional means of attaining scholarship – for example studying in cafes, or at home during unsociable hours, virtually using YouTube and Wikipedia
- Similarly, some less observant Muslims of the daily rituals of Islam, like praying five times a day, may invest a lot more time in checking the halal credentials of food beyond certification, such as expressing concerns connected with environmental issues and provenance that relate to an Islamic ethos. Here, Halal

plays an important role in overtly communicating their Islamic identity and commitment to the faith. It's also possible that this sort of behaviour peeks at certain times of the year, like in the holy month of Ramadan – as a sort of spiritual 'big push'.

THE HALAL PARADIGM – PRE CONSUMPTION DECISION MAKING

On another level, Muslims can be seen to select brands in a different way, which is governed by their interpretation as to what is Halal – according to traditional and modern interpretations and practices.

Muslim consumer behaviour and corporate practices point towards perspectives that are reframing the Halal – towards risk reduction and maximising positive inclinations through overt labelling and symbols.

I present my Halal paradigm model as demonstrating the process of *Think-Feel-Do*. This is an area where *Cognitive* (thinking), *Affective* (feeling) and *Conative* (doing) decision-making patterns are affected by risk minimisation and are dependent upon each other – but may in fact happen in a different sequence, depending on the level of involvement and engagement that the branded offering elicits and necessitates.

Also, ideally you want to elicit pleasure maximisation.

Essentially, this is where you are attempting to elevate the *permissible* (Halal) into the *unmissable*.

These factors are subject to a Muslim consumer cultural lens and their interpretations of Islam. The Halal paradigm is a nub where the perceived importance of Halal is brought into Muslim consciousness. This is a dynamic and cyclical process, whose final verdict is finite and perishable – due to hypersensitivity and environmental factors influencing Muslim perceptions of what is Halal.

In short, consumers search for:

- Textual Evidence (based on current and prior experience)
- Contextual Evidence (based current and prior experience)
- Deductive and Inductive Rational Thinking
- Emotional Inclination and Intuition

Key terms:

Moulding & Fusion of thoughts and emotions [*At-Tala-zum*] – This is a Halal heuristic (trial and error) hybrid-deconstruction approach. Collective individualism drives value-based judgements, derived from a laddering process – as a result of a synthesised hierarchy, and is reflective of a self-defined decision tree.

You will find that various Muslim consumer segments will arrive at the same conclusion via different routes. So you need to establish what factors govern how they reach this point of readiness to consume. A one size or approach will not fit all, but you do need to strike the balance as to how you can cluster Muslims into sufficiently viable and homogenous groups.

Think about it like this. You may have lots on Muslims on an airplane flying to Jeddah to go on pilgrimage - but why are they really going? Why now? Why that plane? How important are those various things and experiences during the entire process, and how do they make them feel? If you took the time to ask, you would find out that there are a variety of reasons why. This is no different to why someone has chosen to visit your restaurant, or buy your particular lipstick. Is it to cheer themselves up, treat themselves, make a new start, meet new people, raise their status, or nostalgia? Actually, the list is endless - but you have to

HALAL DECISION-MAKING
PARADIGM OF MUSLIM CONSUMPTION

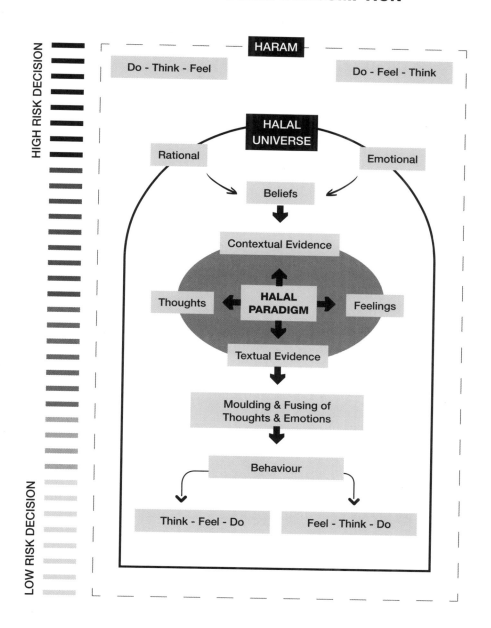

establish clusters of common factors, drivers, and preferences and then rank them.

You also have to remember that the significance and order of these things is dynamic. How we are in the past, may not be how we are today, or in the future. The best brands however, are able to engineer and control these elements, so that behaviour becomes predictable. This in turn enables you to brand-build, by attaching your brand to these various factors, to strengthen bonds of association and eventually drive Brand Reputation and Loyalty.

At-Talazum is Arabic for joining together, with inferences towards fusing and moulding. It is used in an Islamic context to describe the correct approach and mindset for a Muslim to adopt.

THINK   **FEEL**   **DO**

Think-feel-do – This is very much a Halal value-chain approach. Every stage and component is scrutinised rationally, according to their functional and materialistic elements, how these are linked, and which necessitate textual justification.

Feel-think-do – This is more of a Halal cultural artefact approach, where emotions, instincts, and peer-practises nudge opinion. The resulting feelings, emotions and behavioural traits of collective consumerism ratify the validity of an approach.

The heuristic deconstruction stage is the rate-determining step in all of this, which is difficult to achieve over the short term, as it necessitates stakeholder engagement – in

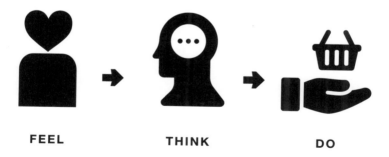

FEEL   **THINK**   **DO**

order to weave brand messages and anchors into consumers' decision-making tree and mind maps.

The value-chain approach represents the safest and most common brand position, appealing to rationality - however it does restrict creative brand expression.

Whilst the cultural artefact approach offers greater opportunity for emotive brand strategies, both tactics still run the risk of opposition and scrutiny – through offering an absolute position of prescribed purity. With Halal ingredient branding and overtly branded Islamic products, such as finance, they tend towards brand messaging with evokes *think-feel-do.*

Nevertheless, a more human, emotional, and friendly strategy of brand messaging that engages all of the senses remains the most effective, yet sadly a currently under-used approach. Therefore I would encourage you to give further consideration as to how more overt emotional messages can be transmitted.

SCOPE AND SCALABILITY OF THE HALAL PARADIGM BEYOND ISLAM

Furthermore, the Halal paradigm can be applied in a wider context – to those with faith and indelible beliefs, which prevent consumers from the conscious consumption of

PROFITING FROM PROPHETHOOD IS A MUSLIM THING

certain commodities.

To this end, the same principle can hold for practising Christians, Jews, vegetarians and other single-issue groups, amongst others. I also argue that this level of perspection is indicative of a new-age marketing approach, which concedes that consumers cannot be coerced with either transactional or relationship marketing methods, without conceding that there are boundaries and limitations defined by the consumer.

Just to remind you: according to Islamic principles, Halal is the norm and Haram is the exception. Within the Halal paradigm of consumption attached to consumerism, this is increasingly being reversed – due to a trait of risk aversion, which is attached to fear and suspicion. I cannot emphasize this point enough. Reassuring consumers as early as possible, through as many communication channels and locations as you can, using a Gestalt of words, symbols, images, signs, and context is vital.

BRAND EMOTIONS, MUSLIMS AND ISLAM

Moving forward, a key area for discussion is what emotional elements are acceptable within the Halal paradigm, how can they be evoked, and to what degree can they be deployed.

Few Halal brands appear yet to be able to satiate both

the rational and the emotional beyond mere functional and materialistic interpretations.

For example, emotions such as seduction and humour appear to be contentious topics when discussed in connection with Islamic brands.

If overtly Islamic and Halal brands are to take centre stage, within the psyche of the Muslim consumer and beyond to a wider global audience; they cannot be neutered and sanitised.

However, this is not to say that they have to sell their souls in the process. Islam and Muslims were once romanticised about by Western orientalist writers – seduced by the mystical, spiritual, sensual, and yet scientific allure, which satiated all of their senses.

Halal brand thinking quite simply means hitting all three pleasure centres: *Physical, Intellectual, and Spiritual.* This is where *At-Talazum* occurs - in that the rational is fused with the emotional.

In the next chapter, we can begin the journey of creating Halal brands.

GETTING YOUR BRAND HALAL READY

CHAPTER FOUR:

GETTING YOUR BRAND HALAL READY

CREATING MUSLIM BRANDS

Having considered all of the previous points raised, the prevailing key question is, *'what differentiates a Halal or Muslim brand?'* Within this question lie several interesting and critical conceptual arguments.

Current brand thinking and approaches are driving for the humanisation and personification of brands – so that successful and emotive brands become, behave and inter-act as if they are living humans. This encourages consum-ers to have deeper, intimate and more meaningful relation-ships with the brand and by extension all of the associated products and services on offer.

If this approach is embraced, then it highlights the fact that Islamic branding has its limitations, as opposed to the idea of creating Muslim brands. Islam is a belief system and a way of life, whereas a Muslim is a person that practices Islam.

Therefore Muslim brands follow the same school of thought as those encouraged by contemporary mainstream branding practice. Furthermore, it is likely that consumers will be more sympathetic and accommodating of Muslim brands, as they are not claiming to be perfect – something which Islam is held to be.

Islamic brands face strong scrutiny from the faithful, for good reason – and so it makes more sense to engage and collaborate with target audiences as friends. This makes for a more meaningful brand proposition, which also allows for more cultural embedding of human personality traits.

As an extension of this approach, a worthy exercise would be to consider projective questions such as:

- Is the brand male or female?
- If the brand went out to dinner, what would it order?
- What music (if any) does the brand listen to?
- What hobbies does the brand have?
- What are the brand's favourite animals?
- What temperament does the brand have: cheeky, shy, cute, chatty, etc?
- Where would the brand go on holiday and what would it do – lie on the beach, extreme sports, visit art galleries, etc?

These brand traits can then be embedded into the brand, its positioning and communications. The value of this exercise is that it makes media promotion choices, creative approaches, language and communication, and target audience selection and engagement much easier – as all of the information is clearly documented as part of a strategic vision.

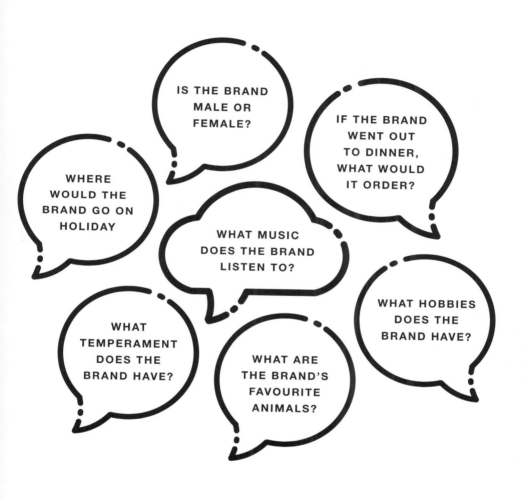

Figure: Excercising projective questions about a brand

ISLAM BRANDED COMMUNITY

Brand

IDENTITY
PERSONALITY
ISLAMIC SYMBOLISM

AFFORDABLE LUXURY
A PROMISE
CULTURAL ARTEFACT
ISLAM FRIENDLY

Non-Muslim   **Muslim**

ISLAMIC BRAND COMMUNITY

Muslim Brand

LIFE-LIKE
ANATOMY
PHYSIOLOGY
IDENTITY
PERSONALITY
ISLAMIC PURITY

AFFORDABLE LUXURY
A PROMISE
CULTURAL ARTEFACT
MUSLIM FRIENDLY

Islam friendly   Muslim

If you've got this far in following my approach, then you should be amassing a vast and eclectic style guide full of stories, anecdotes, images, songs, sounds, smells, objects, colours, places, key people, articles etc – that are at your disposal, when needed and collectively paint a bigger picture that represents your brand's Image, Identity, Personality, Community, and Positioning.

TREAT HALAL BRANDS LIKE REAL MUSLIMS

If we consider the Halal element in all of this and continue with the analogy of a brand being human-like: then think of brands in terms of being born Muslim, or becoming Muslim.

By this what I mean is that some companies from the outset are Islamic, or Muslim-owned and are producing commodities that are Halal. Their challenge is to formally brand them as such and communicate these credentials as being central to their identity.

Alternatively, other companies may decide subsequently that they want some or all of their commodities to be Halal. This *conversion*, like when people convert to Islam, requires slightly different and additional communication. In the early stages it may mean using more Islamic, and Muslim-centric cultural symbolism.

Think of the recent white Muslim convert with the non-Muslim name who decides to wear a topee (knitted Muslim prayer hat) and tasbee (prayer beads) round his neck. Some may even go further in wearing Arab thobes or Pakistani shalwar kameez clothing to signal that they are welcome members of a particular community. Over time, many feel less of a need to rely upon these objects, as they gain in confidence and are recognized in the community.

Regardless of which category you fall into, both types of brand, born Muslim or Muslim convert, like people, have to demonstrate a continuous declaration of faith and practice – in order to succeed. Linked to this, is an ability to exude being confident, comfortable, and authentic – which ultimately lies in the hands of your stakeholders. No amount of professing this without favorable responses can tick this box.

THE THING ABOUT RELIGION IS...

Whilst conceptually and culturally, brands and branding have always existed, brand theory as defined in business academic writing has largely hailed from the west, until recently. Just as the Ancient Greeks and Romans, Arabs, Indians and Chinese have collectively laid down many of the fundamentals of mathematics; I argue that marketers are in a middle passage of learning – which necessitates the same cross-fertilisation of concepts. Branding in particular, due to its ethereal qualities, will pose even bigger problems when trying to understand what brands can do and how they manage to do it.

If Halal brands are to take centre stage as a global force across segments and beyond to non-Muslims, you have to construct and amplify their emotional brand anatomy and physiology. A brand is a promise and your brand's reputation is based upon the fulfilment of that promise – and if you want people to sit up and take notice, you need to inject a touch of swagger.

So as I have suggested, rendering a Halal brand as analogous to a Muslim, rather than Islam is the way forward. This aligns thinking with current schools of mainstream brand thought, which frame brands as being like humans.

Much has been written about the 'Holy Grail' of branding and the iconic status of brands in the modern world. Within the language used lies the allusion that powerful brands are western-centric and marbled with Christian symbolism and underpinnings.

More recently, terms like 'Avatars' open up thinking towards other religious belief systems and eastern perspectives. However, a key question remains as to whether these concepts can be applied to, or embrace the rise of Halal branding and Muslim consumer behaviour?

Therefore, the first challenge when creating Muslim brands is that many of the terms and concepts which exist, are used and resonate in the psyche of individuals are absent of overt Islamic terminology and concepts. This may in fact limit development.

It is also worth considering whether this means Muslim brands have to be created within existing terms and concepts, or whether a leap of faith should be taken to develop new Muslim-centric terms and concepts – which then necessitate that the marketplace has to be educated as to what they mean, and where the differences lie.

A brand is created with the aim of transcending the tangible boundaries faced by a product. The Nike *swoosh* has been one of the most requested tattoos in the USA – and this is not only evidence of this, but in addition proves that consumers feel free to adapt or separate the brand from the product in some way; and extend their level of communication and consumption of the brand.

Furthermore in this case example, the permanence of a tattoo goes towards explicitly demonstrating that the brand can be of more significance and desirability than the product. It appears that brands can develop sublime characteristics, which outlive their associated product.

Successful brands are created with the intention by their owners, of encouraging consumption, patronage and the formation of a relationship - which it could be argued ultimately craves their worship.

So much so, that with their increase in importance, some brands have both individually and collectively managed to attain 'god-like' statuses, which poses challenges when considering that deifying anything other than God [Allah] is seen of as a sinful and un-Islamic practice.

Driving this movement, has been a trend of drawing from, aligning and blending religious language, rituals, mythology, symbolism and meanings - in order to gain deeper significance and competitive advantage. This has either been embedded within the brand itself, and/or through supporting marketing communications messages.

Clear examples again can be taken from the Nike brand, which takes its name from the goddess of victory. In 1997 Nike also faced opposition when one of its trainer designs had to be recalled, as a logo on the shoes resembled the word *Allah* written in Arabic. Here are indications that Muslims are passionate about their faith; able to mobilise global vocal opposition; and are sensitive about how their faith is used and represented.

INTERSECTIONALITY IS THE SECRET SAUCE... BUT YOU HAVE TO FIND THE RIGHT BLEND FOR THAT **SECRET RECIPE**

In tandem, there is an established notion in relationship marketing theory, which draws from a metaphor ascribing interactions between companies and customers as being an engagement in a form of a marital relationship.

As an extension, this has also been adopted when looking at brand relationships. It would appear that this contains within it certain weaknesses, due to an inevitable distance, asymmetry and brand polygamy between parties.

Furthermore, as brands increase in strength and polygamous practices within society are on the decline, it is possible that the terms of engagement associated with branding, may stretch the definition beyond being rooted in a comparable manifestation of a marital relationship.

Perhaps here Muslim brands can offer an alternative proposition, where the polygamous consumption of several competitive brands can be accommodated and reframe what brand loyalty means. I don't want to stress this point too heavily, because my personal view is that trying to elicit brand relationships of this nature is a step too far. I don't really want people to feel married to my brand!

Having raised the issue of worship, it is worth considering some traditional definitions of key terms:

worship: as being, an extravagant respect, or admiration for, or devotion to, an object of esteem – which can take the form of a religious practice, with a creed and rituals.

god: as a being or object of supreme value, believed to have more than natural attributes and powers which require, or encourage human worship. More specifically this can be taken to be the ability to control a particular aspect or part of reality, and/or a person or thing.

polytheism: as being rooted in the belief that there are many gods. Often these gods originate from human and social functions, abstractions of the forces of nature, and objects.

fan: an enthusiastic devotee. The etymology of the word most likely stems from *fanatic* - marked by excessive enthusiasm and often intense, uncritical devotion.

Even within monotheistic doctrines, there is the suggestion that humans have a propensity towards comparable polytheistic practices, whilst however being discouraged. In the Abrahamic monotheistic faiths, worshipers are commanded to worship one deity.

The word 'gods' is usually interpreted broadly to include not just other religious deities, but non-religious concepts and persons as well. Muslims are reminded on numerous occasions within the Qur'an and supporting religious texts, such as *ahadith* of the ease by which they may in fact behave as polytheists.

It has been claimed by some academics however that the attitudes towards celebrities are unrelated to religiosity. Instead, this is more about an idea of compartmentalisation. Compartmentalisation is when we take beliefs and mentally separate them from their unpleasant consequences. This allows us to maintain positive feelings about ourselves by detaching ourselves from the unpleasant consequences.

For example, it has been suggested in some studies that Christians can believe in the story of the Good Samaritan, but detach themselves from the responsibility of behaving like the Good Samaritan.

As an extension of this, the same idea can apply to brands and comparably to celebrities. Whilst many studies examine the beliefs of Christians, these traits can be extended to include worshippers from other faiths. However in doing so, research and analysis should seek to reflect more pluralistic definitions and build on a broader base of tenets of faith.

In addition, as part of a polemical discourse, religious counterparts sometimes draw parallels with the rituals and objects of desire cherished by atheists and agnostics.

Examples of which lie in politics, sport, music and celebrities, amongst others. Notable examples are present when studying the reverence shown by fans of such individuals as Elvis Presley, Michael Jackson, Madonna, Bob Marley, Tupac Shakur, Kanye West, Taylor Swift Jay-Z, Beyoncé, Kurt Cobain, Jim Morrison, David Bowie, Prince, John Lennon, Lebron James, Usain Bolt, Cristiano Ronaldo, Lionel Messi, Vladimir Putin, Barak Obama, Benazir Bhutto, Eva Perón - the list goes on…

Previous studies also present findings of Star Trek fans organising, recruiting and holding ceremonies/conventions, with fan bases that resemble religions. Furthermore this appears to stretch to inanimate objects, where consumers have queued up overnight to purchase the latest Apple handset or sports jersey - despite already being able to fulfil many of the functions, through existing product offerings.

An alternative perspective argues that fame can be interpreted as a quest to preserve a unique part of life for eternity – which applies the concept of a belief in the hereafter. Such arguments extend this to liken celebrity worship to religious worship.

Evidence of this lies in the illicit acts of some celebrities being ignored, mentally deleted, mitigated, or even forgiven - as they are judged according to different value system, which raises their status beyond the common person. This in some way is a precursor to a path of deification. Furthermore, alternative studies have found similarities between religion and celebrity worship in their psychological and physical demonstration of obsessive compulsion - manifest in surrounding rituals and daydreaming.

In connection with worship, an interesting point to note is that the term *fan* appears to have less of the negative connotations associated than with the word *fanatic*, whilst they share the same common root. It is suggested that this diminutive form (fan) hides drivers that would be considered undesirable and needing palliative care.

In addition, fanaticism is increasingly being associated with religious worship, and especially Islam, regardless of whether a formal religion is part of the equation. Therefore in defining consumers as fans, they have always lain roots in stimulating excessive enthusiasm and often intense, uncritical devotion - if unbeknownst to the consumer.

From these definitions, I suggest that resonant brands do experience a form of worship and following this, by the very nature that consumers consume more than one brand,

HALAL MEANS 'PERMISSIBLE' - BUT YOU'VE GOTTA MAKE THE PERMISSIBLE UNMISSABLE!

this worship reflects polytheistic tendencies.

As brands actively associate and create offerings with exemplars of human and social functions, abstractions of the forces of nature, and objects: they will also guide themselves towards being perceived as being more god-like.

This phenomenon of brand worship is a desirable and necessary trait, but at its very least is perhaps unavoidable amongst the most engaged consumers.

Therefore there are two key challenges that Muslim brands face. Firstly, the process of creation of a compelling Muslim brand should be the same as for any other brand, but the intention of the brand creator has to be in line with Islamic principles. That means that having a brand that is designed not to contravene Islamic design ethics and symbolism is not enough - the intentions of the designer also have to be correct.

Secondly, how the brand is promoted and communicated requires care and attention. Fans and worshippers of Islam are things that can be encouraged by a Halal or Muslim brand: but in the process, if the balance of fanaticism strays too much towards the worship of the brand in question, then this will impact on the credibility of the brand itself.

These two points are in fact extremely difficult to manage – because a less than compelling brand will be ignored. Also, it will not only fail, but will also fail in encouraging a greater good and engagement with Halal, Muslims and Islam in a more positive way – which has to be a core ethical principle.

Following on from previous discussions concerning the creation of the perfect Islamic or *Muslim* brand, another point worth considering is what perfection actually means.

Perfection is perishable and subjective - and bound by context, space and time. A good example to illustrate this point can be observed in Japanese culture. Traditional Japanese culture craves porcelain-white flawless skin, hidden from the sun - whilst popular Japanese culture encourages some of the younger generations to chase golden brown suntans, or even obviously fake 'orange' tans from a bottle.

Conversely the Japanese aesthetic concept of *wabi sabi* is lauded when appreciating gardens and ceramics. *Wabi sabi* guides people towards assessing beauty in terms of the impermanent, imperfect and incomplete. Withered leaves, half opened flowers, cracked glazes on pots, and purposefully created wobbly crumpled irregularly shaped ceramics are all seen of as being prized possessions. So perversely, perfection can also be achieved through the celebration, appreciation and acceptance of being imperfect.

To further complicate matters, consumers are likely to have multiple and changing perspectives, which differ

ARABIC IS THE LANGUAGE OF ISLAM, BUT NOT ALL MUSLIMS CAN READ OR UNDERSTAND ARABIC…

**ENGLISH IS THE GLOBAL LANGUAGE OF BUSINESS
AND IT'S INFLUENCING HALAL TODAY**

between brands - what works for one brand may not work for another.

SEVEN WAYS TO BUILD HALAL BRANDS DIFFERENTLY

Here are my suggestions as to how adopting a Muslim branding mind-frame could differentiate you from the conventional western-centric standard. They are also my contribution to debates concerning how Halal Brand thinking can contribute to wider Brand theory and practice:

1. Employees should stand side-by-side with their Brand and live the Brand Experience. Conventional brand-thinking argues that you only have to brand something which your target audience identifies with.

2. Muslims have large referral groups and families who play an active part in decoding brands. Therefore, word of mouth and verification (like in the Islamic tradition of narration chains and ahadith) needs to feed back into brand building much earlier, in order to develop customer intimacy, rather than encouraging customer distance and worship.

3. Think carefully about how you signal honesty and modesty. Accept that you or your brand are not perfect. Rather, brand strength comes from communicating how hard you both try to be the best that you can be.

4. Your focus is on the here and now, but has to be linked to accountability forever (this life and the hereafter). I published a paper proposing Customer After-lifetime Value as an addition to Customer Lifetime Value.
5. A wider commitment towards celebrating beauty across ethnic and social groups, and values-based equality.
6. Loving for others what you would love for yourself. The levels of customer consumption and brand loyalty should be in line with your own.
7. Inspired by the teachings in the Quran.

Many of these brand values are not unique to Halal Brands, but I believe that Halal Brands should make a commitment towards taking the lead in these areas.

THE CHALLENGES FACED WHEN CONNECTING HALAL TO BRANDING

When looking specifically at the role of *Halal* in branding practices, current literature indicates literalist and uniform definitions of what is Halal largely housed within product marketing. However, Halal, as a concept, contains within it attributes which render it both a phenomenon and a noumenon.

In addition, Halal as a concept cannot be fully encapsulated only within these constructs. Brand theory puts forward the proposition that a brand can be separated from the product and service in that: name, personality, identity, relationship, etc. can be created separately from the offering – and in doing so this expands the collective meaning, purpose and consumption of the tangible and intangible entity.

For example, following basic Pavlovian and inductive principles: irreverence, seduction and desire can be the attributes of a brand, which are then grafted onto the functionality of a product or service – resulting in the creation of an irreverent and seductive object of desire.

Within the Halal industry, it should be Islam and more specifically Halal which assumes this position conceptually, rather than any corporate or product brand. Therefore, this renders Halal as the definitive factor, instead of being part of branding strategies, which create something that is Halal.

Whilst it can be argued that the same brand rationale is observed and practiced in the expanding Halal sector, Halal from its classical definition does not allow for this completely. What is Halal at its apex is that which is pure, praiseworthy and of benefit.

Therefore, for Muslims, it should be a given and present in all consumed commodities. An argument can only be made for the Halal if the intention of those involved is sound and it guides consumers towards a way of life (*deen* in Arabic) which is Islamic.

For Halal brands: brand theory should always be cross-referenced, endorsed, or cancelled out by an Islamic standard, which whilst progressive and open to interpretations, remains absolute at its core.

Furthermore, this will render brands conceptually, which align themselves with Halal, in a state of duality and perishability. To this end, marketing communications and branding comes under scrutiny.

If they do not encourage and nurture what is Halal: they may remain as cultural products, but the status of being Halal is temporal. The implications are that Halal ingredient brands may have separate life cycles, which spawn the launch of new further ingredient brand creations. If commonplace, this defeats the purpose for which they were created.

More acutely, Halal in business is often taken to mean what is permissible and needed at every stage to be explicitly asserted, rather than taken as a given. There are numerous optimistic and pessimistic inferences that can be gathered from this that I have mentioned.

In addition, these processes are having an impact on the meaning of Halal, shifting it towards being a business commodity, away from a spiritual ethos.

The knock-on effect is that rather than a tool, Halal could

become a resource draining distraction.

In pursuit of short-term gains, the implications over the longer term are that Halal may cease to deliver the same levels of intrinsic value, pushing the pendulum towards another strategic branding approach and new more meaningful terms that resonate with consumers in the same way that Halal used to.

Having raised these issues, it still remains contentious as to what makes something a Halal brand? The following positions are reflective of differing perspectives:

- Positive assertion by the organisation, through the brand
- The nature of the product or service offering
- Country of origin
- Destination of the brand
- The faith of the corporate owner(s)
- Halal ingredient certification
- The share of Muslim- and Muslim/Islam-friendly consumer base
- The share of Muslim employees
- Positive citation of Muslim-friendly consumer and employee policies/practices; and
- Islamic or Islam-inspired symbolism and messages.

STAFF KNOWLEDGE & CAPACITY BUILDING

As an ongoing activity, you need to ask your staff to consider the following four points in relation to them as employees, the product/service offering, and most importantly the brand. The more that they can establish how more of these qualities and attributes can be transferred into the brand, then the stronger your brand building will be.

1. So how do we develop this expertise further?
2. How do we get recognized?
3. How do we become indispensible?
4. How do we make competition irrelevant?

As part of this process, I would encourage Brand Managers to share this code of best practice with their staff and find ways to communicate them as part of their branding activities, as opposed to just being a Human Resource Management exercise:

- We need to refer to our brand game-plan regularly, and to document and diary everything mapped to this
- We need to learn when to plug-in and when to plug-out of what's going on around us in the marketplace, in trade press articles, with competitors, and in popular culture – and to identify where brands play a part and are visible

GETTING YOUR BRAND HALAL READY

MUSLIMS WORSHIP ONE GOD, BUT THEY'RE ACTUALLY REALLY DIVERSE

- We need to learn about what makes people happy and to find ways that we could try to serve their needs as early as possible – and communicate this through our brand
- We need to improve the way that we identify and solve problems, and find people who can do the same too – and document this as part of our strategic branding framework
- We need to celebrate other people's successes and say thank you often, in public and private – and this should be a component of our employer/employee branding that helps to humanize our brand
- We need to stay hungry to learn new things and to put our learning into practice, and to reflect upon, revise and update what we thought we knew – and find ways to use this in order to refine and refresh our brand
- We need to work hard to complete our tasks early enough, that we have space to dream and focus on the long-game – so that we can maintain a brand that is dynamic, reactive, and futuristic
- We should think deeply and seriously before making decisions, but not take too long or feel regret. Asking for permission or making sure does not protect us from having to pray for forgiveness from time to time

– because our brand is not only in our hands, our stakeholders can and will take control, and otherwise we risk having a brand dinosaur

- Learn when saying no, politely and respectfully, is the best thing, and have no regrets – our brand can't be anything and everything to everyone all of the time
- We should dedicate ourselves to learning the rules of the game, and then start thinking about how we can change the rules to slant towards our best qualities – so we create our own lane, and that's what will deliver a unique and influential brand
- We should entertain and encourage the idea of creating for want of a better term Personal or Employee Brands, so that people can find us, remember us, and know what we do - quicker and more easily than without that identity. A corporate and product/service brand is the sum-total of all of our endeavors – they don't tell and sell themselves
- If we keep doing this for long enough then it demonstrates a proven track record and creates a brand – otherwise, all we are left with is a name, a logo, a commodity and a distant memory
- Don't think about money too soon - think about legacy, and when we look back what we want to be

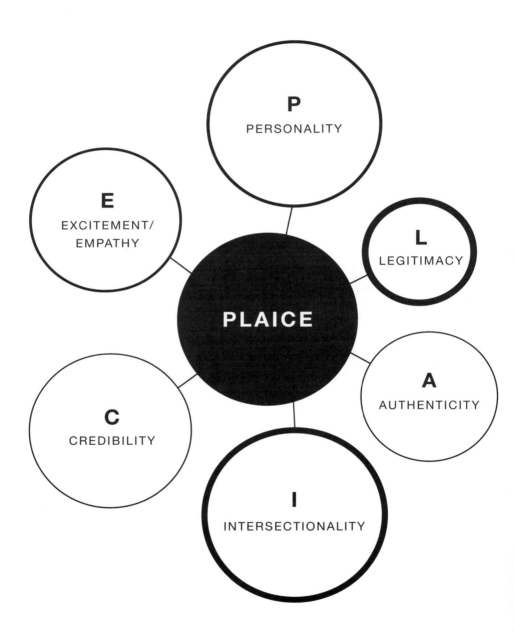

GETTING YOUR BRAND HALAL READY

remembered for. Probably, many of the people that we look up to and respect weren't as acclaimed in their times as they are now...

- Be our own worst critics – it's better that we find the faults, rather than others. But don't let this stop us from living or let it break us.

YOUR BRAND-READY HEALTH-CHECK

Once you have gathered all the information that you can and considered these points, then you should step back and look at the bigger picture to evaluate whether your company or personal brand are able to deliver the following 6 elements:

PLAICE:

- Personality
- Legitimacy
- Authenticity
- Intersectionality
- Credibility
- Excitement/Empathy [depending on if it's proactive or reactive]

This is the new age of iterative transparency in thought and action. Information is no longer faceless – we're giving a face to the melting-pot of globalization. It's also a more emotional activity – sharing who you are, where you are, how you're feeling, and what you're about matters to people more than ever.

This is the 'T-shaped' approached to knowledge – where you cover both breadth and depth. Being a general expert has never been more important and it reminds me of when we were back at school and had to study a broad curriculum. But at the same time people are looking for domain experts who can deep dive into particular areas.

Collaboration now means that you probably have intense experiences with a diverse group of people according to region and sector, surrounding a particular topic, and then once that's been thrashed out, everyone moves on and forms another group tackling the next topic on the horizon.

In the next chapter I will dig deeper into how you go about creating a Brand and developing a Brand Strategy.

05

CREATING A BRAND AND BRAND BUILDING

CHAPTER FIVE:

CREATING A BRAND AND BRAND BUILDING

Everyone is talking about branding and talking in brands – and why not?! Beacause of all the areas of business, it seems to make sense to focus on your brand. If you get it right, then what you have to offer stands out and can command a premium. If you get it really right, then it weatherproofs your activities from recession, it can allow you to carry over equity and brand currency into new product lines and markets, and your brand may just become a word that enters the dictionary as a new verb or noun – to Google or Wiki [instead of doing an internet search], iPads [instead of tablet devices] and Hoovers [instead of vacuum cleaners]…

By the end of this chapter I want you to associate these keywords with brand-building: *Recognition, Relevance, Reverence, Reputation, Celebration, Monetization.*

ISN'T BRANDING EASY?

On one level, it's very simple. It's so simple that everyone gets what brands are and that you have to do it. Everyone has a view on branding and gives it a go. It's fun, gets our creative juices going and it makes what you are doing seem real and unique.

People believe in branding so much that often the first thing they do after coming up with a business idea is to give it a name and to see this as the brand. That's the job done, right? Wrong!

If it was that easy, then all brands would work and would be successful – but we know that isn't true. Names do matter, but how much? If we see the US President as a brand and take former President Barack Hussein Obama as an example: before he was elected, I bet that name would not only be at the bottom of the list; but also many would have argued that his name is so wrong in the eyes of the average American that it could prevent him from being elected.

So actually, does the name really matter that much? Yes it does - but what is more important is that the meaning behind it, surrounding it, and what you do to control, frame and maintain that name's meaning in the minds of your stakeholders is what really counts.

So every man in a kopitiam [Malaysian coffee shop], mom and her cat has a go at branding. That makes it tough for professionals to communicate their expertise and value, even amongst colleagues. Every business wants to own a killer brand, but how many want to invest the necessary funds to make that happen? Because brand building, at the very least, takes planning, time, continual refinement, persistent reminding and most likely money.

I have a PhD in Global Branding and Culture. It meant spending 3 years:

- Reading about 1,000 pieces of work in the field from over the past 55 years
- Personally interviewing and analyzing the views of a diverse panel of carefully selected experts, from industry and academia, from around the world who worked on 185 brands across sectors
- Interviewing the same people several times over a period of 18 months - because I shared my findings with them to see if they changed their views
- Writing this up into a PhD thesis that is close to 100,000 words
- Creating my own theories.

My doctorate is available as a free download from the British Library. If you read it you will notice that I also draw from the work of Aristotle, Plato, Socrates, Al-Ghazali, and Ibn Khaldun. Now you might be thinking that these aren't the names of the usual brand gurus that you hear of – but I was convinced that within underpinning Brand theory and practice there are basic universal philosophical principles, logical arguments, structures, and ways of questioning that you need to understand.

You will find many conventional definitions on what a brand is and does – but what I want to do here is present my key findings in a more easy to digest, straight to the point and practical format.

THE CULTURE OF BRANDING IS A HUMAN TRAIT

One of the conclusions from my PhD was that Brands and Culture are two key things that define human existence. In addition, our free will and ability to change the language and meanings behind these brands and cultures further differentiates us from all other creation. Whilst there are many modern definitions, labels, and terms that are used to help us understand what Brands and Culture are and do - Brands and Culture have been with us for a long as humans have been on the planet. We have always created names and symbols, and linked them to objects, people, regions, experiences, and of course religion. This has been part of our pursuit to communicate more meaningfully, classify, and in many cases establish a hierarchy rooted in emotions.

When you say that your name is Hanifa, which means in Arabic an upright believer in the oneness of God; you're the daughter of Ahmad, meaning the praised one; you are from a line of doctors, originating from Pakistan; you have a degree in quantum physics and work as a data scientist for Google in London; you like Tom Ford Private Collection oud, Mexican food, Adidas Originals old school trainers, zebra print hijabs, Manchester United football club, New Zealand All Blacks Rugby, the boxer Muhammad Ali, Malcolm-X, and Jimi Hendrix – then what you are doing essentially is communicating in a way, punctuated with pockets of tacit meaning, that sends signals and conforms with brand theory.

For it to be brand theory in practice, then what you have to do is formalize these activities within a strategic framework, link them together, and continuously reinforce, amplify, and repeat them until it's abundantly clear to others who you are, what you are and what you're about - whilst having to use less and less words over time.

WHAT IS A BRAND?

Branding is one of the most popular business courses in business schools now. Students all over the world are signing up and business people are picking up books off the shelves of airport shops to sharpen up their thinking and practice.

So if you read the proliferation of branding books, blogs and articles on the market, then we will all tell you that:

- You can brand anything - and I genuinely do believe that
- There is an art and science to brand creation and build-

"Brands are meaning creators, language shapers, and game changers - designed to send a clear signal, which can be converted into social and economic value. A brand has to bring you more money, power and respect than without it. It has to make you easier to find, understand, love, trust and forgive than without it."

CREATING A BRAND AND BRAND BUILDING

ing – which I call the art in science and the science in art

- A brand is more than a logo – it could even become a cultural artefact that outlives the functionality of your offering. For example, Sony's *Walkman*
- Brands have an identity and a personality and brands are becoming more human than they ever have before – we interact and relate to them in a very emotional way
- Brands are memes – an element of culture passed from one person to another by imitation
- Brands are emotional first and rational second – just like humans
- Brands, like people are perishable and paradoxical, and that can actually add to their attractiveness – just like people
- Branding is all about storytelling – and the best stories have a purpose that resonates with its audience
- Stand-out brands should be attractive, exciting, experiential, immersive, entertaining and intriguing – no matter what the industry or your offering
- Stand-out brands are usually able to convert this conspicuousness into success and sales
- Brand-building is all about relationship building among all stakeholders

- Brand communications are better when they teach – and not when they breach or preach
- Brands are defining and framing communities and tribes
- Successful brands today embrace co-creation and seek consumer involvement
- Consumers are taking power away from brand managers and that makes branding more tricky
- People are increasingly seeing themselves as brands
- Nations and cities are also looking into branding themselves, in an increasingly competitive and global landscape
- Branded causes help you to go viral
- Branding doesn't mean shouting louder and being more conspicuous – it's about right place, right time, right tone, with subtlety and sophistication.

You might be surprised to hear from me then that in some ways I think it's time to put textbook definitions of what a brand is to bed.

Now, I'm not saying that you should stop reading these books - but eventually you need to go further and deeper. If you want to replicate a winning brand formula, then by reading these books essentially you are following a recipe in the same way that you would if you were reading a cookery book. They can give you structure and form to your brand strategies and fill in the gaps. This may be enough in the beginning.

However, it's worth remembering that brands are different to dishes, as they are influenced to a much greater degree by complicated environmental factors - such as time, personality, your culture, technology, market forces, and at what stage you enter the market. Furthermore, for many of you reading this book, you will be searching for a way to deliver a unique selling point and value proposition. Therefore, I want you to think about answers to the following questions:

- What do brands mean to you?
- What do they do and how do they do it?
- How could they do it differently?
- How would you do it differently?
- What does it for you in terms of being a great brand?
- What would make your brand average and instantly forgettable?
- What is a definite no-no and a brand killer?
- What promises can you credibly offer, with consistency?

From this you'll get a sense of me encouraging you to gather as much information as you can, to reflect, and to do this constantly – but eventually you have to develop your own style, blend, and flavour.

Be selfish: after all, the best brands are authentic, credible and truthful; and so they have to have something of you in them – your fingerprints, footprints and experiences. You have to capture those things and rest assured that if you do this well enough, then eventually they will be much more difficult for others to replicate.

So a brand doesn't start with a name, it starts with an ontology (your world view and philosophy), a personal mantra that drives your manifesto, and a narrative.

At this stage, I've purposefully not discussed the Halal element or factor. Many brands in the Halal space fail because they don't consider their core brand elements and view Halal as some sort of secret sauce or X-factor. Remind yourself that Halal means *permissible* – and that's not enough to build an exciting branded identity and personality.

HOW DO YOU DO IT?

Do you need to be qualified in branding? Most aren't - but you do need to train. It might help if you look at it like this: guitars are instruments that anyone can pick up and get a sound out of. Many of the great guitar legends taught themselves. Also, being able to play the guitar doesn't mean like Barry Manilow said that you can "write the songs that make the whole world sing". Okay, granted, crooner Barry is a slightly cheesy reference: but that lyric encapsulates what we want to achieve with our brands and branding – *make those brands that make the whole world sing.*

So once you've picked your brand 'instrument': branding takes practise; and you have to decide what style and genre you want to perform in. Like in music, some fields do require classical training and qualifications, but others need you to let your hair down and not be too caught up in the establishment way of doing things.

Most importantly, your success is going to be defined by how you connect with your community. And success isn't all about making money upfront, or attracting large numbers – don't sacrifice the desire to 'keep it real'. As one rapper put it, "feeling satisfaction from the street crowd reaction".

Looking at the previous example of Hanifa: if you were to tighten those elements and pockets of information up – then you could actually create a formal brand and do brand theory.

The important points to note here are that:
1. Branding is about active dynamic two-way communication – you have to think in real time and several

steps ahead, if you want to control your image

2. All brands are linked, classified and categorized in the minds of your audience – inside and outside of your sector, whether you want them to or not

3. So brands and branding are about joining pieces of information together – and then navigating and controlling that process

Brands essentially have to fulfill these four basic functions:

1. They have to give you stand out – in terms of visibility, recognition, reputation, uniqueness, and top-of-the-mind awareness

2. They have to increase your value, desirability, reputation, and equity – or put it another way make you more money than if you didn't have them

3. They act as a cultural container in which you can gather all of the important and relevant aspects of what defines who you are and what you do – and you can then present that package to an audience in a way that they can understand and digest easily

4. They have to give what you do a cultural position, context and relevance.

...And these have to be things that whilst supported

by other activities, can only be achieved through your Brand and Branding.

This is why I describe successful Brands as being:
Meaning creators, language shapers, and game changers.

I am going to give you two stories as an alterative way to understand branding:

In the story of Pinocchio, he was a puppet created with the desire to become human. When you create a brand, it begins its life as a slightly wooden puppet. Your desire should be to make your brand as human as possible, so that it can take on a life of its own – and that will enable you to interact with stakeholders in a more meaningful, deeper, and rich way.

In the story of Goldilocks, she tried to eat porridge that was too hot, too cold, and just right. If your brand is the porridge, and Goldilocks represents your customers, then the challenge for you is to make your offering available, enticing and intriguing – and following this, find out what makes your offering 'just right' and tasty.

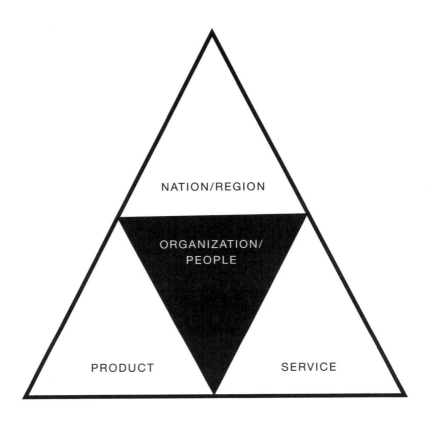

BRANDS LINK YOU TO A BIGGER PICTURE AND CREATE OPPORTUNITIES

It doesn't matter whether you want to do Nation, Corporate, Product, Service, or Personal Branding – you need to see these things as being linked. For example:

- If you offer a service, then adopting the strategy of branding it and extending the offering to something, which also has tangible branded products, strength-

     CREATING A BRAND AND BRAND BUILDING

ens not only your business, but also your brand

- If you're doing Nation Branding, what top branded products and services come from your country?
- If you're an organization, what value does it add to your brand that you come from a particular nation or region?
- If you're a personal brand, what tangible products and intangible services do you offer, and is there a clear and consistent link with these offerings to you?

I also want to stress the point again about governments, companies, or individuals believing that they have a brand and they are doing branding – when in fact what they may have is a logo and the potential to build a brand.

Let me use this scenario to illustrate my point:

Hafsa wants to create a Personal Brand. She goes to see a graphic designer who agrees to help her out. She creates a stylish logo using the letter 'H', with a cute lioness cub leaning against the letter (because Hafsa means little lioness in Arabic). It looks great. Does she have her personal brand now? What happens next?

...Well Hafsa's left thinking about whether this logo is going to help her make more money and allow her to charge more for the things that she wants to do - like sell cupcakes, hijabs, vlog, and offer consulting advice to people who want to understand more about Muslim females like herself. She soon realizes that the logo can't do much on it's own. She has to bring the brand to life.

She shows the logo to her friends and no one knows what the logo means. People don't know what's so great and unique about what she's offering. They can't see the connection between her lioness and cupcakes, hijabs, vlogs, and consulting – in fact how are those activities linked to each other regardless of the logo? How is she able to prove that she can do the things that she says she can, and where can people verify these claims?

She's not sure how she should promote herself, where to go, and whether she should do so in a way that tackles her competitors head-on, or avoid such aggressive tactics. Also, she has no idea how she should communicate with people – should she be serious, religious, spiritual, funny, or cute?

In the way that I've presented this scenario, it should be clear that the logo isn't where her focus should be – rather she should be thinking about what will enable her to get recognized, stand out, communicate a clear and consistent message, and ultimately charge a premium for her branded promise. Branding is a vehicle for unified communications.

It might also make you reflect upon how many businesses say that they have a brand, but can't answer some of the questions that Hafsa faced. This means that they too will face similar problems. If you don't actively control your brand and people's perceptions and relationships towards it, then it will remain weak, drift, and offer little in the way of added value.

All of these questions should lead you to thinking that brands require a plan, timetable of activities, and a strategy. The logo is the start of the branding journey and this is where Brand Managers take over. I would argue that a good Brand Manager, like an Advertising or Public Relations professional, can work with almost anything and dramatically change the perceptions of how a logo appears. Ultimately, the test is whether they can increase Brand Equity – the value of a brand and what price you are able to command.

HAVING A NAME AND A LOGO DOESN'T MEAN THAT YOU HAVE A BRAND

If we apply the learning from Pinocchio and Goldilocks: then this means that creating a commodity, name and a logo isn't enough to make it a brand – it's just a puppet and part of the story. Similarly, branding isn't about being bigger or shouting louder than everyone else – there is a just right approach, which whilst maybe having the same ingredients as others, in many ways is unique to you.

Once you start to produce a series of strategic messages continually over time and get these messages right - then people, through association, will start to recognize your logo and pull those meanings into the logo by proxy.

This signals the journey of your logo becoming a brand. The greater the depth and number of strong associations linked to your logo, the stronger the brand you have – in very much the same way as people grow in reputation and status.

THE SIXTY-FOUR-THOUSAND-DOLLAR QUESTIONS

Just like with people: your brand will be judged by the company that you keep. But don't be fooled into thinking that it's just about sharing content and getting your brand everywhere. Keep a handle on the bigger picture – why are you doing all of this?

- What do you want to win: eyeballs, likes, shares, authenticity, loyalty, sales? You need to be strategic and balance being responsive in your messaging with a long-term mission.

Now, unless you have a meaningful and intimate relationship with consumers and clients; or your message is bang-on – just being in the right place, at the right time, in the right tone isn't enough. It's no longer cool to mass broadcast and tell consumers what to do.

I also mentioned to an audience of 5,000 marketers in Jakarta, Indonesia in December 2017, that old social media thinking is very macho - in that it seems to be about being M.A.L.E.: Making, Audiences, Like, Everything… when it should be more F.E.M.A.L.E.: Focus, Enhance, Multiply, Amplify, Legacy, Energize. On the face of it, framing mindsets according to gender traits seems like simply an eye-catching headline tactic. However, I will discuss this area in more detail later on in the book.

So:

- What do you think people will sense and piece together from all of the images and information that you're pumping out? The most important views are going to be tacit and you may only get glimpses

SHARES?

EYEBALLS?

LIKES?

WHAT DO
YOU WANT
TO WIN?

LOYALTY?

AUTHENTICITY?

SALES?

CREATING A BRAND AND BRAND BUILDING

of them – so you need to be reflexive, intuitive and connected.

What you can do is to group all of these into answers that form the foundation of all of your strategic communications. If you take a step back - is it clear to everyone else:

1. **What is it that you do, and do differently from everyone else?**
2. **What your overarching story is - that builds credibility, curiosity, intimacy, likeability, and excitement?**
3. **What you have to offer them – both tangible and intangible?**
4. **What you want from them, or want them to do?**

I call these four questions your elevator pitch – short statements you can deliver on your website, in a corporate or personal profile, in a pitch, on a package, in a campaign, at a job interview, or whilst exchanging business cards. People have a short attention span and this has to be done quickly and attractively, without talking things up.

Surprisingly, when many people are put on the spot, whether that's representing a brand or themselves, they can't. Most people can comfortably answer half of the first question: 'what is it that they do', and then they trust that their name or branded existence will offer them enough differentiation. If you were then to ask the other three questions, these same people may struggle to offer suitable answers. Often people essentially repeat the same answer that they gave to question one.

If you think that you can respond appropriately to all four questions, then still keep your eyes open and an open mind – because there's probably someone out there doing it better than you that you could take some inspiration from.

The more specific you are the better. Generalist rhetoric like, 'I am a Muslim and I want to make a change to humanity' isn't good enough. For example, if what you have to offer is a fizzy drink, then your good intentions could easily be misinterpreted as being unrealistic, sensationalist, or even insulting.

The more you think, practise, and share; and the more that you do this exercise in such a way that you can still be yourself, a better 'self' - then you improve your chances to succeed and cut through the noise. Don't do this alone in isolation - align yourself with consumers, stakeholders, and other brands by creating a network.

The elevator pitch is something that you will have to do time and time again until you have a strong brand where it speaks for itself and consumers speak on your behalf.

BRAND-STORMING CHECKLIST

Firstly, you should consider each of the following points and be able to provide concise answers to each of these questions. This is your extended elevator pitch. It may help if you are able to write answers to these questions that fit onto PowerPoint slides – as a series of short bullets.

Audit/Analyze/Evaluate

1. Know your Lane

1. What exactly it is that you do?
2. What is unique about what you do and your offering?
3. What benefit(s) and value do you offer your customers?
4. What and how do you want your customers/stake-holders to behave and act?

2. Know your Range

1. What are you good at and what do you not do?
2. What do you do that could be stretched to serve sup-porting markets?
3. What audience clusters are your compatriots?
4. What regions do you serve?

3. Know your Level

1. What volume, frequency and timeframe do you deliver your products/services?
2. What quality level do you deliver on consistently and at scale?
3. How sacred/mundane/profane is your product/service offering?
4. What size does your organization operate at?

4. Know your position

1. Where you stand in terms of being evolutionary or revolutionary?
2. Do you seek to innovate or renovate?
3. Are you serving or creating needs and markets?
4. Do you want to position yourself as the market leader, number two, value proposition, niche copy-cat, boycott alternative, ethical choice etc.?

You should strike the balance between being factual and injecting an element of poetic writing. I like to write short copy which at times rhymes and reads like billboard copy – however, you have to be careful that if you are going to be more creative in your writing, you don't lose the message, by replacing jargon with words that aren't clear in explaining exactly what you do.

STRATEGIC BRAND FRAMEWORK

Many companies that I have come across believe that completing this task signals the end of the strategic branding process – and that's a mistake. Strategies have to be revisited and refined time and time again – especially as the landscape and potentially your business is changing constantly. The keywords here are framework and process. Just like football managers have game plans, the best managers are able to adapt and respond when they see further opportunities or face unexpected challenges.

Therefore, the purpose of a brand strategy is to gather information, appraise and process it, and then find a way to engineer and communicate this information in a more sophisticated manner, with as few key points as possible. This means that:

1. You need to re-work your answers into emotive and attractive words, slogans, phrases, sentences, and stories. The order in which you present these can affect how successful you are

2. Find infographics, images, sounds, textures, and even smells that can replace some of the words – with the purpose of de-cluttering and enriching your communication. With repetition, these supporting elements will begin to be associated with your brand.

THE 3 STAGES OF THE
BRAND LIFE-CYCLE

CREATE

BRAND
- Anatomy
- Physiology
- Essence
- Humanization

MAKE EVERYTHING HUMAN

CURATE

- Market Proposition
- Stakeholder Engagement
- Context & Position
- Social Currency

CENTRE OF COMMUNICATION

Branded Culture & Cultural Brands

SHAPE CULTURE

CULMINATE

The following models contain components that I believe have to be present in a compelling brand offering. You should be able to demonstrate as precisely and clearly as possible where these elements are present and how they deliver for the brand.

THE 3 STAGES OF THE BRAND LIFE-CYCLE

Powerful brands are those that are iconic, charismatic, authentic, effortlessly cool, that take you on a journey. These brands cross the Rubicon into becoming *meaning creators, language shapers and game changers.* They seek to engage with everyone that they come in contact with in as human a way as possible. They trigger emotional responses that guide your thinking and actions.

They act as vessels, containing our messages and offerings, which sail the seas of our social oceans on a voyage culminating in a catharsis of intriguing and intense experiences. Those are the moments that capture your attention, make you want more, and want to share.

For me, there's nothing wrong with being passionate and persistent about introducing people to your brand and encouraging people to want it and share it more - this is an essential pursuit of business. However, there is a difference between doing so with the right intention, in an honest way and going to market with valuable propositions - to encouraging mindless consumerism with deceptive and exploitative practices.

All too often, brands get a bad rap, and unfairly so - because of one or two brands that underperform, disappoint, or go too far. I think it's also worth reminding ourselves that nothing is so black and white and everything is branded - from countries, to political parties, to people, to even theories. Therefore the key consideration for any brand and especially Halal Brands is how to get the balance right.

I've used poetic language here on purpose, because there should be something at the start of your brand's creation that elicits daydreaming. This will make storytelling easier - encouraging you to be more creative and enjoy the brand-building process.

For those of you that have experience in raising children, then you know that there are fun jobs and ones that aren't so much fun. Whilst you worry about the day-to-day things, it all seems worthwhile when you look to the future and remind yourself of the bigger picture.

Day-to-day, I have to say that there are two favourite times of the day for me in parenthood – breakfast and bedtime stories. If we relate that to branding, then breakfasts (like brands) are limited in terms of choice, simple to put

WHAT/WHERE/WHEN/HOW/WOW?

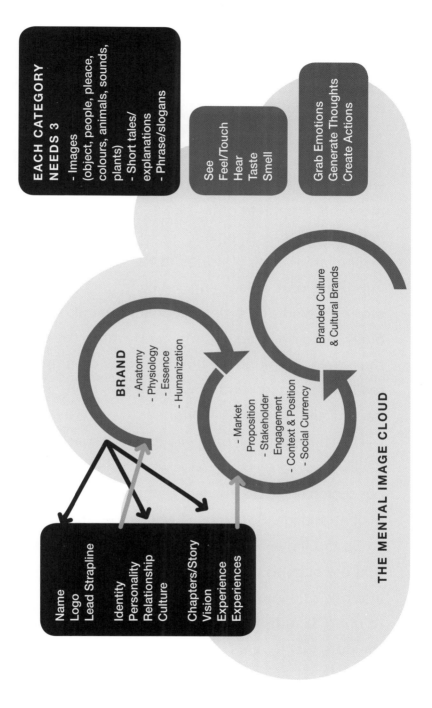

EACH CATEGORY NEEDS 3
- Images (object, people, pleace, colours, animals, sounds, plants)
- Short tales/explanations
- Phrase/slogans

See
Feel/Touch
Hear
Taste
Smell

Grab Emotions
Generate Thoughts
Create Actions

BRAND
- Anatomy
- Physiology
- Essence
- Humanization

- Market Proposition
- Stakeholder Engagement
- Context & Position
- Social Currency

Branded Culture & Cultural Brands

Name
Logo
Lead Strapline

Identity
Personality
Relationship
Culture

Chapters/Story
Vision
Experience
Experiences

THE MENTAL IMAGE CLOUD

together, not meant to be your only meal and shouldn't take over your whole day. You have to get up and running, get on and get your brand out there.

Likewise, you shouldn't spend all of your time creating a brand (like a breakfast) at the start and think that this will be enough to fill you up for a long time - you have to move on, complete other tasks, and you will get hungry later on for other things.

Similarly, reading stories at the end of the day are an important part of learning, relaxing and dreaming. By stories, I also don't mean reading business press. Seriously, read children's stories and watch the effect that they have. Think about how the rules of language and reality are broken and how these can have a profound impact and increase resonance.

Now bring yourself back into the Halal space and consider how boring many Halal brands are – and yet we would love for our customers to desire them as their most cherished objects of consumption. So you don't want to be a boring brand.

On the flip side, there are so many children's stories that are starved of ethnic, cultural, or religious diversity – in terms of names, characters, or scenarios. If you were to bring all of those things together, then your brand has the potential to stand out and present something that is both familiar and unique.

The approach I am presenting is about an immersive process of cultural osmosis – which is the free flow of high concentration culture into culturally absent spaces. If you create something that is culturally rich, then it will spread.

This means blending the arts with science, drawing from familiar themes, capturing moments of serendipity, and distilling eclectic experiences into one cogent identity, story, ecosystem, with an emotional call to action.

All of this is more than stamping your logo on a product or service, or in a media space right at the end. It means working upstream and downstream towards creating a holistic brand ecosystem. It is also about heritage building and creating a legacy. You need a corpus of stories, sensory eliciting images, packages of communication, and arenas in which you can transmit them.

From this way of thinking that draws in all of the senses, you can see how celebrities find it so easy to model themselves into becoming brands and also transferring this into new businesses. They communicate a place or origin, how this has shaped their life, a reason for being, ups and downs twists and turns – but overall a progression of development towards excellence, and success through achievement and association. Also, excellence in one field is read as being transferrable into other connected or even unconnected fields.

I strongly believe that the same theories and processes can and do apply to corporations, products, services, nations – it's just a little more complicated and tougher, largely due to the amount of work that has to be done to humanize the brand and generate an emotional consumer response. This is often why some companies decide to sponsor individuals, events, products and services that elicit more of an emotional response - in an attempt to psychologically graft these emotions onto their offerings.

This school of brand thought could also be applied to you and me. I mean how else are you going to standout when it comes to applying for that job, or making that business pitch? It's not enough to rely on your qualifications and current job title, or the logo on your business card. A quick search through LinkedIn will show you that we're all easily forgotten amongst an ocean of profiles and logos.

One observation I've made is that Personal Branding has always been at the centre of the message and movement of Islam - with the Prophet Muhammad (peace be upon him) being the best example. One of the names that he was known by was *Al Amin* - Arabic for 'the trustworthy' and this is key to his success - and any brand promise.

However, when we look at the Halal Industry and Muslim origin brands, there are few personal brands, or people that actually use and embrace personal branding strategies, which is disappointing - but remains as a potential market differentiator and competitive advantage. Instead, they focus on sales, ingredients, certifications, and quoting religious scriptures – but it is people that build trust, empathy, and growth.

Whist you have Gates, Jobs, Zuckerberg, Branson and others - post 9/11: Muslims, business people, and entrepreneurs are worried about being so open and socially media active. They have a fear of being a rabbit in the headlights, or tall poppy syndrome – where they will be forced to tackle tricky questions on race, religion, and politics, from a suspicious media outlet, or worse from within their own community: and that will kill their brand.

In such a climate, it's questionable whether we could ever see such characters again like the boxer Muhammad Ali, for example.

However, I do believe that over the next few years, we are going to see a new wave of Muslim brands, underpinned by strong Personal Branding, which are more than halal logos, halal certificates, Islamic artefacts, and Muslim cultural symbols.

Mainstream trade press is reporting that *Brands have to take a Stand* in this post-truth, fake news age - where consumers are cynical, vocal, and influential. Recent success stories of this new way of thinking are LUSH cosmetics, and LEGO. Some have written that activism has replaced sex as being the way to build brands and sell – I think it will be *Sexy Activism* that sells. That means a more sophisticated approach to tackling taboos, which whilst splitting audiences, will strengthen a brand's reputation, authenticity, and uniqueness.

So I do think that we are going to see brands that have Muslims at the centre and surrounding them; bringing in a more human, cross-border, emotional, and sensual (with subtlety) element – we have to, due to the population sizes and demographics that point to them being a youthful, opinionated, and growing community. Couple this with general traits amongst Generation-Z, who for example are drinking far less alcohol, are more culturally aware and globally connected, and we can see where the trend is going.

One thing that I think we will see in business is the revival of the Muslim tradition of a narration chain, and this will feature in business - to demonstrate authenticity, trust, transparency, and provenance. This in a social media age will then cross-over and influence the thinking of mainstream brands in the same way that the Americans, Japanese, and Germans have, with their own culturally-based concepts as a by-product of political struggle and social unrest.

The next chapter will shift our focus towards the psychological dimension of piecing together these various brand elements and traits that you have created.

06

BRAND CULTURE, PSYCHOLOGY & COMMUNICATIONS

CHAPTER SIX:

BRAND CULTURE, PSYCHOLOGY AND COMMUNICATIONS

Brand positioning is all about controlling the narrative. Therefore, in this chapter I am going to focus on Culture, Storytelling and Psychology. A brand strategist's job is to shape consumer behaviour, and to give Marketing, Advertising and PR professionals foundations upon which they can build, enrich and amplify the brand. When I think specifically about Halal products and services, or even people's perceptions of Halal, especially amongst non-Muslims, then these are areas that I feel a lot more work has yet to be done.

DO NOT UNDERESTIMATE THE CULTURAL DIMENSION

Culture and Marketing make us human. Without culture, can there be any such thing as marketing? Without marketing, does culture survive? In the widest sense, we are all producers, consumers, and marketers of culture.

More so now than ever, we have become cultural hybrids and surrogates – where traditional classifiers such as ethnicity, nationality and class say less about us than our possessions, language and social networks.

Also, looking at the rise of the Muslim world and Asian influence, are we moving away from a world of Mad Men towards one of Ahmad Men? [joke]

In the face of these changes, what new Eastern-centric approaches can we use to reinterpret realities? Furthermore, much of our cultural understanding and study in business is rooted in Western notions and constructs of nation, society, gender, obligation, spiritualism, collectivism, and context.

But, in the Middle East and Asia, if we investigate Western notions of masculinity and femininity for example, they can mean very different things. So much so, that perhaps these variables make comparisons difficult. For example, I'm sure that you have seen bearded men from the East, greeting each other with kisses, wearing sweet fragrances, kohl around their eyes, sarongs, and jewelled rings, for centuries; or businessmen with brightly coloured cute charms hanging from their smart phones. And yet, 'they' too are cultural chameleons that can change according to their environment.

These behaviours remind me of the story *The Lion, the Witch and the Wardrobe.* People are seamlessly travelling between worlds and changing their identities in a way that is veiled and concealed from those uninformed and in the dark. Think of the Asian international student who travels to the West, to a different reality, and then returns home, only to hide some of their life-changing experiences.

Hail the dawning of a more Eastern, feminine, softer and sociocultural approach to marketing. Putting others first and fulfilling their needs is the pathway to self-fulfilment. Welcome to globalization and a world of cultural complexity.

As you've probably worked out by now, I'm fascinated by *culture*. I've spent most of my life trying to understand all of these 'things', issues and interactions that we attribute and attach to that word, Culture. I've often found that many people express how important culture is. But fewer are able to articulate these feelings in a strategic and structured manner; and even fewer can do so with any depth across several cultures, to the same degree.

This section hopefully, will give you food for thought, suggestions of ways that you can investigate culture in its various forms, and also a selection of cultural building blocks, which will allow you to break cultural ideas and concepts down in such a way that they're easier to explain to others.

Rohner[5] notes that for many parts of the world concepts of *society* have become synonymous with those of a *nation*. Rohner goes further in asserting that the concept of a *nation* is a *Western* one, originating from circa the nineteenth century – where boundary setting has become more about political expediency, rather than to separate neighbouring societies.

Therefore, I argue that analysing separable sub-cultures linked to national identity, rather than simply nationality, becomes more significant when attempting to understand culture, and especially those outside of the West.

Holden[6] comments on the fact that definitions of culture have only continued to increase, rather than generating a polarisation in thought. Over sixty years ago, Kroeber and Kluckhohn[7] registered 164 different definitions of culture. From these, they find that the *essence* of culture is present where:

- Members of a system share a set of ideas and especially values
- These are transmitted (particularly through generations) by symbols
- Culture is produced by the past actions of a group and its members
- Culture is learned
- Culture shapes behaviour and influences our perceptions of the world
- Language is the mediator

Of the many attempts to define culture, I like Herskovits's[8] definition, which is simply that culture *"is the man-made part of the environment"*. Schein[9], as a social psychologist, makes a distinction between *visible* and *invisible* culture. From this he creates three categories:

1. **Assumptions:** which are taken for granted and invisible
2. **Values:** where there is a greater level of awareness
3. **Artifacts:** the visible face of culture, which is not necessarily decipherable, and often therefore misunderstood. Here, it consists of three manifestations:
   a. Physical
   b. Behavioural
   c. Verbal

However, these offer little guidance towards helping us decide what conceptual units allow for making the best cross-cultural comparisons. This is because, values, norms, and practices may originate from different principles and assumptions – which may then limit the number of abstractions and generalisations possible.

Also, this is perhaps why defining culture beyond what could be seen as truisms or basic principles, continues to yield further definitions. However, I argue that it should not be so much about defining culture according to a 'what is', but rather a *'how does'*?

Ember and Ember[10] suggest that the everyday usage of the term *culture* refers to a desirable quality, which is acquired. However in contrast, Linton[11][12] argues that culture is the total way of life, rather than those parts, which are regarded by society as being higher and most desirable. Similarly, Usunier[13] views culture as a *collective fingerprint*, where:

- Culture is the domain of pure quality
- Culture is a set of *coherent* elements
- Culture is entirely qualitative
- There are no 'good' and 'bad' elements of a particular group
- And therefore can be no *globally* superior or inferior cultures

Anthropology scholars assert that culture is governed by both *society* [organised groups, who depend on each other] and *subcultures* [members who share certain cultural features that are significantly different from the rest of society].

CONSUMPTION-BASED PERSPECTIVE

So, culture is social. And as we socialise, how are we socialising, and with what? Culture is linked to consumption and objects. Objects can be both physical and symbolic. Baudrillard[14] seeks to understand objects not by their functions or categories, but rather by analysing the process where people relate to them, and subsequently the systems of human behaviour and relationships. This supports the socio-anthropological analysis of cultural 'artefacts'. Derrida[15] writes that relationships are best understood through considering the politics of friendships.

I extend the definition of an 'object' to brands and frame the system of human behaviour and relationships to meaning *culture*. Baudrillard states that traditionally, technology views objects as having *essential* and *inessential* structures and functions. In addition, he suggests that objects have a 'language' and 'speech' of sorts.

More than ever, objects are being synthesised to transcend both essential and inessential spheres – and so the separation of these structures is becoming progressively indistinguishable. An example, which Baudrillard considers, is the car engine. Functionally, an engine has to serve a purpose. However, engines are tuned according to acoustics, which evoke psychological feelings of 'sportiness'. Also, furniture and interior decorations comparably fulfil emotional values, which are termed *presence*.

These examples champion the importance of culture in creation, from their inception to consumption – *the man made part of the environment.*

Baudrillard also goes further, in considering *gadgets* - arguing that in the strictest sense, whilst they are objects of desire for many, they actually often fail to fulfil meaningful and sustained functional value. Objects, from Baudrillard's perspective have a primary function of personifying human relationships, *"to fill the space that they share between them, and to be inhabited by the soul"*.

Therefore, I also ague that brands are designed in the same manner as objects and or gadgets, and are being cultured to fulfil wider-ranging cultural obligations.

When examining culture and consumption, McCracken[16] broadens definitions further; to include the processes by which consumer goods and services are created, bought and sold. McCracken[17] asserts that,

"the social sciences have been slow to see this relationship, [between culture and consumption], and slower still to take stock of its significance. They have generally failed to see that consumption is a thoroughly cultural phenomenon...consumption is shaped, driven, and constrained at every point by cultural considerations. The consumer goods on which the consumer lavishes time, attention, and income are charged with cultural meaning. Consumers use this meaning to entirely cultural purposes".

McCracken also cites the postmodern phenomenon of *Diderot effect*[18], which asserts that cultural consistencies exist when a collection of consumer goods are ascribed a characteristic meaning. An example, which McCracken provides, is of 'yuppies' that consume *BMW, Burberry,* and Burgundy wine. More recently, McCracken[19] observes that in a postmodern society culture is founded in transformational activities:

"It is possible we are witnessing the creation of a global self and an expansionary individualism...Individuals claim many identities and a certain fluidity of self – this much is accepted by postmodern theory. (We now accept that identity has less and less to do with things that remain identical)".

Gilmore and Pine II[20], ascribe this movement in business, which is consumer-driven, to the pursuit of *authenticity*.

With such informed and individualistic consumers and stakeholders, McCracken[21] also argues that living, breathing corporations can maintain success, relevance and control through appointing *Chief Cultural Officers.* In McCracken's thesis he highlights that cultural understanding is of the utmost importance to brands and that if understood fully, brands will resonate so strongly that they become part of the cultural fabric of society.

With this in mind, I think it's essential that organizations consider appointing *Halal Cultural Officers* in a similar way.

Therefore, the work of cultural anthropologists and philosophers are highlighting that cultural insight can be unearthed through observing participants' consumption of commodities (physical and symbolic), and most notably now, brands.

Furthermore they appear to support a point made by de Mooij[22] that, *"Instead of causing homogenization, globalization is the reason for the revival of local cultural identities in different parts of the world."*

For example, it would also appear that with branded denim being sold at a high price tag - whilst looking old, worn and distressed (an approach championed by *Diesel*), indicates that brands and commodities are attempting to embed themselves seamlessly within existing cultural usage, whilst also commanding a premium for the privilege[23].

It is this embedding process which is helping to support the argument that brands are orchestrating many aspects of modern culture, as opposed to 'hitting notes' in pre-existing cultural musical scores.

When looking specifically at Muslim Youth, I argue that rather than these individuals becoming '*Westernized*', as has been suggested by traditional quarters, and equally by Eastern and Western sources: Muslim Youth are in fact entering an age of new becoming. This is *the New School of Dual Cool*.

For if this is a simple case of Westernization, does this mean that the 'West is best', and are Youth moving away from being 'Asian', 'ASEAN', 'Arab', 'Pakistani' etc or religious? Or is it that they see their identities as being governed by their own rules, which are open to inspiration and truth wherever it exists?

Evidence for the last perspective lies in the increase in visible practice of Islam by Muslim youth – most notably in their dress and the conversations on the Internet, which are there for all to see. Muslim Youth are consuming commodities that were thought of not to necessarily have any Islamic reference or relevance and they are *Islamifying* them. Brands, designs, celebrities, and art forms that have elements which resonate with these Muslim's own peer groups or value systems become adopted and reframed as being Islamic. For example, longer t-shirts that cover sagging trouser waistline gaps, especially when bending down in prayer; pairing maxi dresses with long sleeved undergarments, or wearing Japanese kimonos in preference to more traditional jilbabs; listening to drum driven Hip hop music, and Hip hop inspired Arabic *Calligraffiti* artwork.

In addition, I would argue that East/West, or Muslim/The West thinking harms the development of understanding – as it implies separation. And more importantly by inference supports the idea that the strongest brands, media platforms and educational systems lie outside of the hands and inception of non-North American and European nations, which then profiles Muslims as being intellectually impoverished and followers.

Therefore, if this is the case, Muslims may now and in the future be profiled as romantics who were once great, but now live in the shadow of the enlightened West. Now, these reflections are not unique to Muslims and there are also some European nations that are facing the same challenges. However, a disproportionate amount of media coverage is given to the role of Islam and the positioning of Muslims in the world today. We need to think carefully about the political drivers behind these debates and find a middle ground of being able to decipher what to rebut, reject, and present as alternatives.

I think that business has an important role to play within all of this. Economic growth, education, inclusion, diversity, and social mobility are key factors that we have to consider - and if addressed, will go a long way towards answering many of these questions. In an age of media concision and rankings, citing brand success stories grab attention - whether that's a corporation, nation, or famous person.

ESTABLISHING A CULTURAL LENS FOR MARKETERS

Summarising all of the points raised, they outline that culture is acquired or created - and is transmitted subsequently through teaching and learning. It exists on multiple levels of abstraction. The most significant aspects of which are tacit - and therefore are understood best by those who are the most active in that collaborative process.

Culture is a living breathing language, both verbal and non-verbal, and is symbolic. It is preserved whilst being rooted in the here and now. It joins participants together and presents anchors of understanding.

Having presented these differing approaches and perspectives, my recommendation is that, in a given scenario, culture should be analysed and understood on different interconnected levels – and the best way to do this is to participate.

The following model offers guidance as to how these levels can be categorised, and how they relate to each other.

The diagram should be viewed as a Venn diagram model with 7 variables. In some situations, only one cultural frame of reference may predominate, for example local customs. However, in other instances, several variables may work in tandem or against each other. There may be a subculture, which draws from local customs, or a departmental culture that clashes with organizational culture. So don't think of

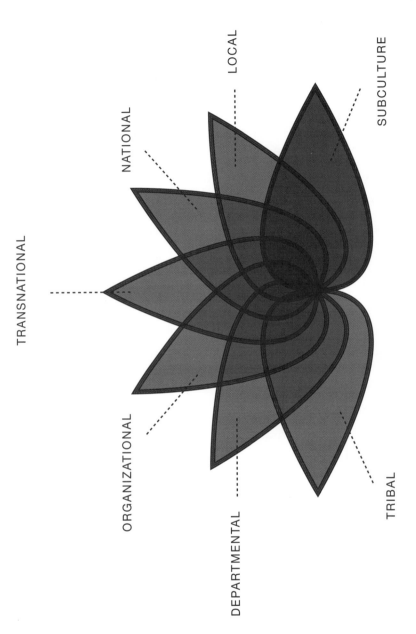

Figure: "The Petals of Culture"

TRANSNATIONAL

NATIONAL

LOCAL

SUBCULTURE

ORGANIZATIONAL

DEPARTMENTAL

TRIBAL

BRAND CULTURE, PSYCHOLOGY AND COMMUNICATIONS

culture as being one thing and remember that to possess culture necessitates being cultured.

Marketers should see where different levels of culture: conflict, join, cancel each other out, enhance, and govern activities. This is an organic, human and communal process.

So, embrace culture... seek it out wherever you can... nurture it... admire its beauty... share your experiences... keep its memories alive... and plant its seeds - so that it will blossom again when the seasons change.

I've laboured the field of culture, because undoubtedly understanding and developing mastery of this area will make your Halal Brand and Branding. Falling short will break your brand and render it obsolete.

This chapter is also meant to highlight how much work is yet to be done on developing a more detailed and nuanced understanding of Muslim consumers, across geographies, cultures, ethnicities, ages and other distinctive and significant traits.

To give you an example, let's focus on the Indonesian Hijabers grassroots movement who are in control, gaining momentum, wider interest and starting to cross-over. The potential of a brand from an emerging market like Indonesia is massive.

DON'T JUDGE A MUSLIM BY THEIR COVER!

BRAND CULTURE, PSYCHOLOGY AND COMMUNICATIONS

For the benefit of the readers outside of the ASEAN region: Indonesia consists of 18,307 islands, has a population of 263 million, 300 ethnic and linguistic groups, speaking 700 languages. Close to 90% of the population are Muslim, making it the most populous Muslim nation on the planet. And let's not forget the 1.7 billion Muslims spread across all continents that share the same faith, which has led to the Muslim fashion market being considered one of the next big things.

So when designers are not being asked to answer questions concerning what modest fashion actually is and means – other considerations are who are the target audiences and how should these items be marketed?

This is where some answers from analysts, in my view, have fallen short and I'll try to explain why.

It's unrealistic to assume that all Muslim females, or headscarf-wearing females will be interested – because we are talking about fashion and the importance of personal taste and style beyond mere functionality. The material, the cut, the pattern, the fit, the price point, premium, and not to mention the brand all play their part.

Similarly, there may be people that support or equally reject the fashion movement, its values, image and identity. This is no different to consumer's views on any culturally linked clothing – be that national dress, right through to sub-culture street wear.

Next, if we tackle suggestions that wider non-Muslim audiences may be interested – they may, or equally may not. Some people may love being associated with Muslim-inspired dress, just like the urban chic trend of wearing keffiyehs (Arab male scarves), which is fused with edginess, rebellion and revolution. Others however may dislike these links and therefore reject such fashion, based on this principle.

Therefore, what I am suggesting is that marketing this scene boils down to some good old fashion marketing intelligence that takes into account the basic segmentation criteria of: *Geographics*, *Demographics*, *Psychographics*, and *Behviourals*. From these, a web and layer of messages, images and associations have to be created – through Branding and Integrated Marketing Communications.

It's not enough to say, let's target Muslim women, say *salaam* and *Ramadan Kareem* to them, charge less money, and provide garments that cover more flesh. There has to be an emotional connection and immersive storytelling going on that helps to seduce consumers and galvanize them into tribes of active brand ambassadors. This is the tough part, as it's nuanced, connected to a cultural zeitgeist, and just as subjective as trying to launch a new music group.

But the designs that have iconic designers who share their emotions and personalities on social media about anything and everything stand a better chance. We need to taste that edginess, rebellion, revolution, and reality.

THINK OF HALAL MORE AS A CULTURE THAN A RELIGION

A better way to view this market is to think in terms of Socio-Cultural Ethnic Marketing. This is more about branding a lifestyle choice, an experience, a scene, a sub-culture, a counter-culture – thriving because it exists outside of the mainstream. These factors give the movement its authenticity, allure, and earthy grassroots feel.

This is also why I drew parallels earlier with Hip Hop and Popular Culture. Whilst the key participants may be Muslims and Islam is their rulebook, the style-guide is coming from their lived experiences and free expression.

Therefore, to lead your promotional activities with an overtly and explicit religious message may not be the thing that first hooks consumers. Invariably, more effective messaging is sophisticated and sparks curiosity. If we fast forward to where Hip Hop is today: you don't need to be African American of Hispanic to be part of the scene - you just need to respect and celebrate Hip Hop's roots. There are no marketing messages that say 'suitable for black and white people', whilst the content and participants might be biased towards one community.

So yes, there are nearly a couple of billion Muslims, and several billion more non-Muslim consumers ready to consume Halal – but please don't view the market as simply as one according to Muslim and non-Muslim. There is a great degree of intersectionality going on outside there, and markets have never been more dynamic and nuanced.

It's also why I am an advocate in a marketing, branding and consumer behaviour context for viewing Halal as a cultural system, rather than a religion.

PLAYING THE COMMUNICATION GAME

Understanding consumer behaviour, segmenting and targeting audiences; service quality delivery; social network analysis; advertising, public relations, sponsorship, and branding; product design and aesthetics; and personality tests at job interviews: are just a few of the areas where marketers are looking to the 'ologies' [anthropology, psychology, and sociology] for insight and to steal an competitive edge.

I am going to focus here on the theatre of communication, offering some building blocks and principles behind what could be developed eventually into a form of game theory - which embraces the playfulness and dynamic emotions that influence our decision-making.

COMMUNITY AND SOCIETY BUILD OUR WORLD VIEW
The dichotomy of Gemeinschaft and Gesellschaft
Gemeinschaft and *Gesellschaft* are German words, used in sociology to categorise social ties:

> **Gemeinschaft** [community] – This is an ascribed status; comprising of a fundamental shared set of values, beliefs, norms, customs, rituals, kinship, behaviours and artefacts that individuals possess, and which binds them to one another – from the sacred to the profane, and through to the mundane. The bonds of Gemeinschaft represent a community of fate, where both good and bad fortune are shared.

> **Gesellschaft** [society] – This is an achieved status built on secondary weaker relationships, where larger associations never take precedence over an individual's rational self-interest. Globalization, business, organisations, employment, and citizenship are examples of these societal relations.

In practice, Gemeinschaft and Gesellschaft work together, forming a blended reality, which changes according to

REPUTATIONS ARE BUILT ON THE FULFILMENT OF THAT PROMISE YOUR BRAND MAKES

time and context. Both are open to abuse: and over-engineering, or the creation of artificial and fictitious qualities run the risk of eroding either category, or swinging the pendulum the other way.

KNOWLEDGE OF SELF - LINKED TO OTHERS
The Big Five personality traits

Psychologists have attempted to describe our personalities by grouping them into five broad categories, which form the acronym OCEAN. This means assessing whether or not we possess qualities of:

- **Openness** – intellectual curiosity, creativity, imaginativeness, independence, a preference for novelty and variety, open to change and new experiences
- **Conscientiousness** – self-discipline, dependability, thoughtfulness, ability to control impulses, and manage expectations
- **Extraversion** – assertiveness, energy, emotional optimism, sociability, leadership tendencies, dependency on others and a breadth of experiences and stimulation
- **Agreeableness** – compassion, cooperativeness, harmony seeking, and trusting

- **Neuroticism** – emotional instability, anger, anxiety, depression, and vulnerability

Not possessing any of these qualities points to an individual exhibiting an opposite trait. So for example, introversion is the opposite of extraversion, and may mean that someone prefers to spend time alone, needs less stimulation from his or her social world, or is shy. Equally, in a certain setting, introversion could be temporary and as a result of neuroticism. The key lies in identifying what is the most common tendency of an individual within a given community or society.

EGO AND TRANSACTIONAL ANALYSIS

Moving beyond the big five OCEAN traits, if we accept that we behave differently from time to time: how does our communication change?

If we look in the field of psychotherapy at structural analysis, people are seen to change and shift between patterns of behaviour, states of mind, and psychic attitudes – known as ego states. These can be reduced to three main categories, which any of us have the ability to enact:

- **Parent** – those traits that resemble controlling parental figures, which are either nurturing or critical

- **Adult** – a neutral and objective appraisal of reality
- **Child** – still-active archaic relics, which were fixated in early childhood – ranging from natural free, rebellious creativity; to adapted, conforming and submissive.

These states are dynamic and become apparent when two or more people communicate. There are two levels of communication: the social level, and on the psychological level. And this explains for example how an adult can behave like a child. Within one conversation, it is possible that someone can switch between states. Communicating is seen as being engaged in a form of reciprocal transaction and for communication to continue, it needs to be complementary, and there needs to be a stimulus.

Now think about how you would classify the following pieces of communication and advertising slogans:

"Sprite – Obey your thirst" [Parent]

"Apple – Think different" [Parent]

"Adidas – Impossible is nothing" [Parent]

"Carlsberg, probably the best beer in the world" [Adult]

"HSBC – The world's local bank" [Adult]

"Nokia – Connecting People" [Adult]

"Audi - Vorsprung Durch Technik" [Adult]

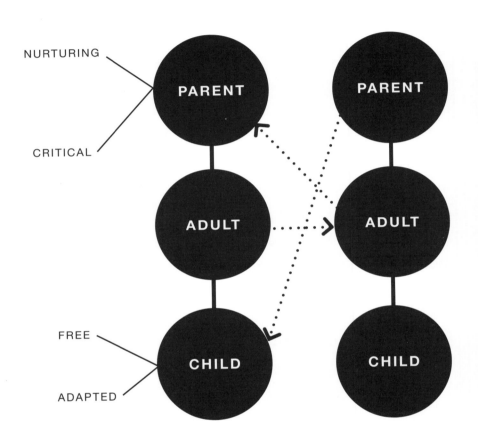

"Nike – Just Do it" [Free Child or Parent]

"L'Oréal, because you're worth it" [Free Child or Parent]

"L'Oréal, because I'm worth it" [Free Child]

"Virgin Airlines - Your Airline's Either Got It, Or It Hasn't" [Free Child]

"Virgin Airlines – Hello gorgeous" [Free Child]

Each slogan conveys a certain personality with its message, but it's also important to remember that depending on who conveys the message, the context, and the style, then the path of the transaction can change. Some of the most iconic brands have used paradoxes, and humour to create a unique and compelling message – especially when eliciting parental or child states. Eric Berne's 1964 book 'Games People Play' goes into this in more detail, and it's clear that more games can be played when people adopt parental or child states. One example he cites is of the salesman who says, *"This one is better, but you can't afford it"*.

THE ART OF LEADING COMMUNICATION - WITH PURPOSE
Rhetoric – the mode of persuasion
Rhetoric is the art of informing, persuading and motivating audiences through arguments. Aristotle held it to be the tool of logic and politics - categorising it according to three

appeals to an audience:

Ethos – How well an individual is able to convince an audience of his or her authority, honesty and appeal on a particular subject. These are the relevant aspects of an individual's character that have the ability to enhance the appeal of an argument. Ethos can be broken down further, into three categories:

- Phronesis – wisdom and practical skills
- Arete – goodness, virtue and excellence
- Eunoia – goodwill towards an audience

Pathos – A communication technique used to appeal to an audience using emotion, passion, stories, hooks, and figures of speech – such as analogies, allegories, hyperboles, and similes.

Logos – The logical reasoned argument, which makes things clear. Logos also enhances ethos. In addition, a simulated argument, where data is manipulated and re-contextualised, could in fact be used to enact a pathos effect.

HOW TO PLAY THE FIELD
The Human Transactional Equation

I've put together the following simplified model - which brings together the various personality and communication factors and categories mentioned earlier that govern communication exchanges.

The idea is that facilitating and controlling communication efficiently, is something that takes practice, pragmatism, flexibility and self-reflection. Effective communication is nuanced, subtle, sophisticated and dynamic. It blends the rational and emotional - reading what can be seen, with sensing and unlocking what is hidden. The best communicators and communication move like quicksilver: they have a form and function – and are smooth, bright, fluid and able to respond to change. This is a collaborative and cumulative process governed by environmental factors. And so, the key challenge is how you're going to shape that environment, whilst keeping communication channels open and positive.

Also, where I have used the terms 'I', 'Them', and 'OCEAN': my thinking is that each can be used interchangeably in the singular, collective and abstract. So any of them could be applied figuratively to brands, a corporate identity, or an object – that is if the human bonds and characteristics are strong enough to facilitate this.

CASE EXAMPLE IN PRACTICE – HOW SOCIAL MEDIA CONVERSATIONS PLAY OUT

Now think about Online conversations. Adult communication tends to be forgotten or ignored - or at least initially. When faced with so many online posts, which encourages us to skim read, you are more likely to notice the ones that express strong emotions first. These grab our attention and often frame debates. Some marketers and media outlets have used this to their advantage, spawning the term 'clickbait'. In essence they are provoking or evoking emotions - even when these are sandwiched with numbers and facts, designed to trigger or claim rational communication. These play into the hands of that form of transactional communication, which Eric Berne describes in his book as 'games'.

Within these games, people are attempting to use a form of controlling language, which exhibits Adult, Parental or Child states. However, a key challenge for a company facing criticism is not to respond in a Critical Parent state - even in the face of provocation, as it rarely goes down well.

Adult or Nurturing Parental states could be used to neutralise strong emotions in a measured way. Nurturing Parent or Adapted Child can show that you understand and care, with empathy. Free or Adapted Child can show your passion and that you stand side by side with the

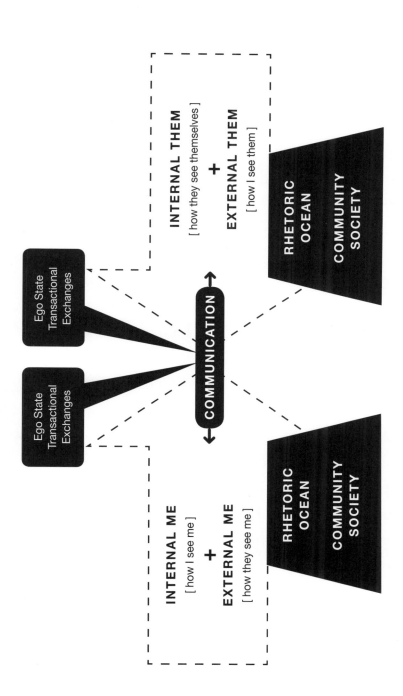

Figure: Personality and communication factors

people you are communicating with.

The Internet is full of people empowered to be free and rebellious with their communication. Similarly, there are plenty of consumers who are ready to step in and adopt a more parental and critical position than the organisation – where the organisation traditionally was thought to be the parent; possessing all the power and legitimacy.

USING STORYTELLING TO ENHANCE YOUR BRAND AND COMMUNICATION ACTIVITIES

Having looked at the various psychological theories and techniques, and how they play out in practise, I want to shift the focus towards how you can prepare for these various forms of communication. Therefore, this section is now going to be more about practice-based skills. The best communication, brand stories, slogans, and explanations are prepared well in advance. Even if your communication is responsive, still you should be drawing from a selection of scenario-based responses, decided and practised in advance - to a level that allows you to do so in real time, with confidence and authenticity.

I've found that whether you're creating something, preparing for a gig, big match or big pitch, the process is actually very similar. Perhaps the only differences are how much time you have to prepare, make decisions, or what you write down as opposed to just thinking them.

WHAT YOU NEED TO DO

Therefore, in the next few pages, I want to fire you up into a state of being immersed in working towards bringing your brand to life, so that you can position and promote it correctly. Your brand will come to life the more you can live your brand. In order to do all of these spot on, follow these thoughts and ideas - so that you can come up with the *who, what, when, how,* and *wow* that will inject cool into your brand. All of these activities will form the basis of your branding playbook.

The more times that you practise the processes and stages I've outlined, then the faster and better you'll get at them, and ultimately quicker at achieving your overall task. They will add structure to your activities, help to build up your confidence, and make it easier to work again and again – even when you feel that you are up against it, or are suffering from a mental block. The key thing to remember is that you are finding a way for your mind to turn this mountain into a pebble, and that relies upon your ability to manage your mind, more than the reality around you. Manage your mind, and the rest of your body will follow.

Think about all those other people, day in, day out, around the world, that are able to do the same in their fields of expertise: colleagues, medical doctors, athletes, rappers, chefs, and many others. If they can, then you can. Remind yourself that you've been asked to do this task for a reason; and that reason is that people think that you can do it, and do it well. Remember all of the times that you've been able to succeed at anything, even when you thought that you wouldn't be able to. Reflect upon how you came out of the other side, able to turn up for work the next day, stronger and more accomplished. Tell yourself that you don't need as much sleep and food as you think. Imagine what it will feel like when you succeed and how others will look at you. Plan how you will reward yourself, celebrate your achievement with others, and convert it into another stepping-stone towards your career goals.

It might sound like an obvious thing to say, but don't panic. Stay calm, start taking some deep breaths, try to relax - but stay alert and keep that adrenaline pumping, but under control. The mark of a professional is being able to handle and channel that pressure in a way that others struggle to do, and to deliver the goods. That also means handing more matters back to your unconscious, rather than your conscious mind. The more that you use your conscious mind, the more tired, slow, and stressed you are going to feel. Think about Olympic sprinters, rappers; or footballers and stand-up comedians reacting – when they're in the moment, they don't really have to breathe or think about what they do. They trust in their training and the unconscious takes over.

Now that you've built up your confidence and started the process of talking to yourself; delving deep into your emotions and memory - the real work begins…

Go back to the task at hand and study what it is that you're being asked to do carefully – it's easy to see something that isn't there, or to add more than is required from you. If it's a 20 minute talk, 10 PowerPoint slides, or an 800 word article, then aim to do no more. Anything more is a waste, and you don't have much time to waste.

You need to draw from your experiences and not reinvent the wheel - you are an expert in something, with experiences and a perspective that collectively no one else has. Think about what material you might already have sitting somewhere on your hard drive, smartphone, and browser history. The key is to link them to the task at hand.

Actually now, go and reinvent the wheel. Well, add something new to the wheel that everyone already knows about and understands - a new perspective, an innovation, something... Something that makes people think; something that maybe they've not heard of before, or at least for a while; share something of your own thoughts and experiences, good and bad; let people into your world.

But make it interesting. Tell us a story – something that you'd like to hear, even if it's not actually strictly your story. The fact that you've chosen to tell that story, and chosen to share it with us, is what makes it special. But don't forget to tell us why you're telling us this story, how does it relate to what's going on here, and what's in it for us? Also, don't make the story too long...

Before you start, you need to get warmed up. Watch TV, whether that's the news, a documentary, a sitcom, stand-up comedy, a movie – whatever gets your brain ticking, stimulates and relaxes you. Phone your friends, surf the net, watch YouTube and TED talks, and absorb what's going on around you. Make notes and draw pictures on paper, or your smartphone and tablet – anything and anywhere, just save them in one place.

Now switch off from the world and isolate yourself. Have a coffee, wash the dishes, iron some shirts, cut some vegetables, go for a walk, do something boring or simple that let's your mind wander some more and process all of this information.

Make some more notes on paper, or your smartphone – anything, but start to write bullets and phrases...

Now put your notes down, go away and do something else - anything…

Now go back and sit down, lock yourself away and write.

Put: who, what, how, when, where, why, and wow at the top of your page.

Write the body first, then the conclusion, and then the intro and title last.

You need pictures. Either that means actual images, or painting images in peoples' minds through your storytelling. If there's an opportunity for both, then great!

Within your work, you need to offer several perspectives. Try three angles as a starting point; odd numbers work better, and remember to tell your audience the number in your list – it makes it easier for us to process your message.

Break things down into several points. Use this as a three-stage structure for each perspective that you present:

- Facts, Explanations and Conclusions
- Or, Conclusions, Explanations, and then Facts.

It may take you some time to work out what flows better; and often the first time you're putting things together, the explanation might pop-out first. However, resist the temptation to miss out a stage and jump to the conclusion part of your explanation, without any explanations. This is all about communicating in a clear, logical and easy to understand manner – no matter what the topic is.

Don't be afraid to pose questions, even if you don't know or provide the answers to everything. This is about looking to connect and engage with your audience. Whether you like it or not, their brains will be asking questions, as they process your information and everything around them; some of which may not be intended by you or within your control. By asking questions, you're bringing them back into your space and your script. Whilst you're preparing and writing, imagine you're having a conversation. Sometimes it helps just record you chatting into your phone.

I'm going to make this point again. Make it interesting. Make it something that you would be bothered to listen to, or read, and share. Link it to what's happening now. The top brands are dynamic and relevant. They find a way to link themselves to stories as they happen. The richer your brand story, depth of communication, and cultural intelligence, then the easier it is for your brand to link to a wider range of stories, with credibility and authenticity.

A REAL EXAMPLE TO GET YOU THINKING

Okay, so you might be thinking about what stories or examples you could use. I mean how far off track can you go, and then bring it back on track? Here's one of my stories that I used in a talk about the importance of cultural understanding in leadership and branding:

So here goes…

Now, we all know that not everything is as black and white as it seems, right? Well, when I was thinking about this point, an image of a zebra popped into my mind. So what about the zebra? Well, here's a question for you: is a zebra a black animal with white stripes; or a white animal with black stripes?

It might seem strange, but that's the first question that popped into my mind. But as an academic, creative and consultant who spends a lot of his time thinking about things and finding solutions, then actually I'm used to my mind asking these seemingly irrelevant questions, when there seem to be more pressing matters.

So, as you might expect, my mind was quick to answer this trivial question. However, the more that I thought about it, I started to become unsure about whether I knew the right answer or not.

What do you think? Let's have a hands up who thinks it's

a black animal with white stripes; now hands up who thinks it's a white animal with black stripes?

Okay, you want to know the right answer, right? Well, I did what any academic would do; I suspended my own judgments for a minute, and went searching through various literature sources.

Well, the answer is – it depends... If you take the position put forward in one academic study, in the field of anthropology, then they will tell you that it depends too. From their findings, it depends on your cultural frame of reference.

It appears that people from Africa, tend to see it as a black animal with white stripes; whilst people from Europe see it as a white animal with black stripes. So I'm sure that you can see how that works.

But, when I've asked this question on my travels amongst various ethnic groups, especially from former colonies, more often than not, they tend to see zebras as white animals with black stripes. So does that mean they have colonized minds?

Think about what impact the culture of today and yesterday has on the way that we see things. Also, think about when you get older, does your hair go white, or does it get darker? Of course our hair turns white. If you take the position of some zoologists, then they will tell you of course it's a black animal with white stripes; because the white stripes are the places where there is an absence of pigmentation.

So why am I telling you all of this? Well I'd like to say that it is for three reasons.

Firstly, not everything is black and white, or black and white in the way that we think.

Secondly, that our culture, experiences, and frames of reference shape the way that we see things; and that may be different to the way that others do.

And finally, that we have the ability to change the way that we see things, if we want to. But this can only happen if we ask questions, no matter how simple or trivial, that it's important to do this both alone and in groups, and through looking for answers in diverse sources.

Once we do this, and we share what it is that we have found, then we can start working out what makes a great leader, or brand – because culture matters, it's everywhere, and it touches everything.

APPLYING THIS TO HALAL

Often, people tell the story of how animals were slaughtered. Think about this for one moment - that's not a story, it's information! Talking about death is a good way to kill the conversation and your brand. Other people discuss what Islam is and how the Prophet Muhammad (peace be upon him) lived. How is that your story? How does it relate to you? Sure, you might want to follow in his footsteps and celebrate his tradition, but this story isn't about you – who you are, what you do, and what is happening today.

Frequently, people use antiquated language when they quote translations of the Qu'ran and ahadith that were first written a long time ago. This causes a disconnect with the language of most modern branding and advertising – which seeks to funnel the here and now into a friendly and engaging format.

Think really hard about speaking about you, your company, and offerings. As tempting as it may be, do not espouse rhetoric of the universal nature of Halal, the religion of Islam, or the Halal industry in general, because it's not strictly your concern and you don't have the budget to do it.

You have to be really selfish in this regard, as you have limited funds and consumers have a limited attention span. I know that this is tough, when you're faced with questions about what Halal is, confusion over so many definitions and interpretations, and so many negative media stories – but these are a distraction, and you should just treat them as people's potential interest in what you are doing. It's up to you to control the narrative.

CONCLUSIONS

Marketing continues to move, evolve and grow at a rapid speed. Promotional activities have to communicate in a way that is both timely and timeless – that's quick, dynamic, diverse, integrated, and viral branded messages, through tangible and intangible media channels. In a social media age, they will be there forever. For people that believe in life after death, that really means forever!

For them to remain competitive and fit for purpose, Halal promotional activities have to be about more than the creation of products and services, which are designed to create or respond to the needs and wants of consumers and businesses.

There needs to be a focus also on the wider values and practices of individuals – and especially those of marketing practitioners too. Professionals should practice what they preach, in a way that is visible to all - seeing the path to professionalism and perfection as being able to walk in the shoes of their audiences, as companions. This shared understanding will help to forge a moral compass, and practices able to preserve values and relevance - whilst safeguarding against exploitation and isolation, which could erode the authenticity, credibility and ultimately viability of marketing activities over the long-term.

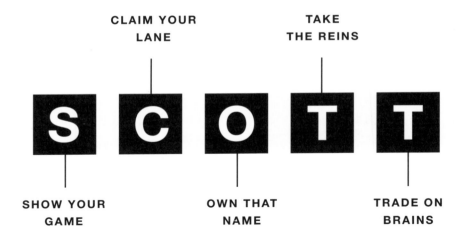

So to round up:

Consider how you would answer each of the following points, using facts, figures and anecdotes. This is the marketing blueprint and style guide that grounds your contributions strategically:

S.C.O.T.T.

Show your Game - that you have a competitive edge

Claim your Lane – where it's clear what you're about

Own that Name – your domain, sector, and personal handles

Take the Reins – make sure that you're in control of your destination

Trade on Brains – demonstrate that you're a connected thought leader

...And do the same again and again

Finally, just to tighten things up even more, refine this information into an elevator pitch. Learn how to communicate in different voices, to different word-counts and styles appropriate for particular platforms and audiences. One-size does not fit all. Inject emotions and, if possible, poetic storytelling to make them more memorable. Finally, bring everything together into one slogan. However, in trying to be poetic, do not make your language or descriptions cluttered and abstract. Stick to the point, less words mean more - instead use objects and experiences that paint pictures in your mind. When Steve Jobs introduced Apple's new iPod in 2001, the slogan was "I,000 songs in Your Pocket". Emirates Airlines launched its aspirational "Hello Tomorrow" slogan in 2012.

The slogans work, because they are underpinned by communication that addresses the points I have listed in SCOTT. All of these things have to work together and need to be ratified by your audience. These things can't happen overnight and are likely to take several years of iterations in order for them to solidify your brand position - whether that's for a product, service, company, nation, or person.

If we now shift our focus back to Halal brands: which Halal brands can you remember, do they have a distinguishable personality, what is their slogan?

07

MARKETING AS REAL PEOPLE

CHAPTER SEVEN:

MARKETING AS REAL PEOPLE

INTRODUCTION

Many marketing and branding books inadvertently place a distance between those who are producing products and services, or creating brands and marketing campaigns, and those who are consuming them. I strongly believe that the best brands and campaigns reduce this divide - and consumers are viewed as and feel like collaborators.

To facilitate this process, branding professionals need to evaluate their mindset, education, and skills competences. Looking further forward, we have to look also at how institutional systems, whether they are organisations or educational establishments, find and shape talent.

If we focus on the Halal space, this is even more crucial, because the Islamic tradition celebrates the importance of the character of individuals and how they interact with others. Islam is built on preserving and narrating the journey of people. However, when we look at Halal, which focuses on day-to-day lived experiences, all too often discussions seem to focus on certification, ingredient credentials and simply what is permissible. I would like to see more character-building branding and promotional activities that excite audiences - and that means nurturing professionals that can carry these forward.

With these thoughts in mind, this chapter takes a broad view on what role marketing professionals play in Halal businesses, language as an art form, how these link to branding, and how we segment consumer interest groups. These following few steps will help you to differentiate your Halal Brand in a sea of logos and tag-lines.

Also, I think it's worth mentioning that I receive a lot of messages and questions from people wanting to find out more about how they can work in branding and marketing, and specifically Muslim majority of minority markets. This chapter has been written with you in mind too.

INDUSTRY AND UNIVERSITY TEETHING PROBLEMS

Going slightly off topic for a moment, I want to share some facts to support why I feel that more work is needed in this area, in theory and practice, and that this is a collective obligation and necessity - part of 21st century living, regardless of faith.

The first major trend that I would like to highlight in the Halal space is the significance of English language and the influence of Western powerhouses. Many of the world's most famous advertising and creative agencies were founded in London during the 1960s and 70s. More recently in 2017, London was deemed the world's most attractive city to companies for the tenth year running by the Tokyo-based Mori Memorial Foundation. The UK creative industry is growing at twice the average of the UK economy, and the UK creative workforce is growing at four times the rate of the UK workforce. I'd also like to mention the *Journal of Islamic Marketing*, launched by UK's Emerald Publishing in 2010, which was the first dedicated academic journal tackling the field of Halal, Islamic Marketing and Branding.

A recent BBC News article reporting the findings of a study undertaken by High Flyers in the UK, cites that graduates who have had internships are three times as likely to land jobs; and Marketing is the most popular sector for these jobs. Advertising and Public Relations are the most desired jobs by graduates, with 50% across the UK planning to work in London and 21% overseas. Furthermore, graduate aspirations of wanting to work in cities like London and further afield are indicators that marketers are seeking environments that are culturally rich and multicultural. Over 300 languages are spoken in London; approximately 45% of the population are White British,

15% are White non-British, and 40% are non-White – what a fantastic microcosm and training ground.

Apart from graduate career aspirations, it could be that the industry demands are greater, and graduates are responding or even being sucked into the profession. Nevertheless the demand is there and the discipline is expanding its tentacles, so should business schools do more to attract marketing applicants – as not all marketers will have studied marketing? And, with such demand, the call for more qualifications in marketing, marketed more widely will surely help contribute to the competitive advantage of individuals and organizations.

Whilst it's undoubtedly an imperative that we bring more ethnic minorities, Muslims, and women into marketing, advertising, and branding professions, without tackling these bigger societal and industry issues, it may not make as much of a difference as experts might suggest. Having started my career in advertising, anecdotally, I saw that some minorities weren't that bothered about challenging the status quo and some put their heads down and kept quite - for fear that it might affect their careers.

The status quo points to these roles being held increasingly by people with a university education. Now, according to the Higher Education Funding Council of

A BRAND TELLS A STORY, PAINTS A PICTURE AND MAKES A PROMISE

England (HEFCE): in 2015-16 UK-domiciled Black and Minority Ethnics (BME) accounted for 29% of all entrants to full-time degrees [they make up 18% of the 15 year old population in the 2011 census in England]. So this is great news in terms of knowledge capital and potential talent, especially in this space.

However, sadly, non-white students are less likely to achieve a first or upper second class degree, even if they enter with the same grades. According to the Higher Education Statistics Agency: for the third year running no black academics have worked in senior management in any British university in the UK. 510 were white, 15 were Asian, and 10 were mixed. Universities employ more black staff as cleaners, receptionists, or porters than as lecturers or professors. Also, The Runnymede Trust reported in 2015 that out of 20,000 professors in the UK, only 85 were BME.

I make these points because the UK has some of the most diverse campuses and highest-ranking universities globally, not to mention some of the most influential advertising, branding, and marketing professionals. So, how knowledge is being taught, how people are being treated and nurtured, and how things are being produced and communicated – all have a significant knock-on effect on how Halal is being marketed and branded.

CHANGING SKILLS

When I was at primary school, what were called the 3Rs – *reading, 'riting* (writing) and *'rithmetic* (arithmetic), were considered to form the basics of a good education. With the advent of social media, reading and writing are definitely key. Perhaps arithmetic to some has become less important - as we have machines that can do those things for us. Also, technology consumption points to the abstract memorization of things and information seeming less important than how we access, link, and use them - in a variety of ways and settings.

We have new skills. For example, typing almost everything, predictive text, speech recognition, and spelling and grammar checkers have changed the landscape. Making mistakes, leading to green and red squiggly lines under words, can in fact be a way of problem-based learning. We have the chance to amend our mistakes as many times as we want, with little fuss, unbeknown to others, and away from their glare and scrutiny. The art of right first time with ink and brush or pen is now just the domain of painters or calligraphers – I haven't written a job application in ink since the nineties. The same can be said for handwriting a full draft

before typing it up – it just doesn't happen any more.

Also, I used to know all the phone numbers of my friends, by memory. Now, I can count the phone numbers that I know on one hand. Predictions by futurologists such as Google's Ray Kurzweil also suggest that by 2040 we will be uploading the contents of our brains onto computers – our entire personality, memory, skills and history; possibly also boosting our brains with processing and storage power. (Metro Newspaper4).

IN TALKING WE TRUST

The Telegraph newspaper reports that UK university admissions staff now rank 'good written English' as the key to a good personal statement, beyond anything else. Kyle Wiens also writes in his Harvard Business Review Blog, titled: 'Why I won't hire people who use poor grammar. And here's why' that, *"Good grammar is credibility, especially on the internet. In blog posts, on Facebook statuses, in e-mails, and on company websites, your words are all you have."*

So, less time speaking on the phone and more time typing - the art of letter writing is back in fashion; but this season's fashion is cut differently. 'Writing' is *typing*; font and typography have replaced handwriting styles; your writing has to be timely, and on the right platform; search and keywords matter; and the tone in many ways has to be timeless – even if it's an instant response. Quick communication that's there forever.

THE ART OF TALKING THROUGH TEXT

The apex of the Islamic tradition revolves around the words of the Quran and the Arabic language from which it is comprised. The poetic nature of the verses are praised for how they sound and the way in which they invite people to reflect; they have been used visually for art and calligraphy; and the grammatical structure of sentences have been used to derive legal interpretations, through deduction and induction.

Halal branding has to bring all of these style elements and depth together, along with contemporary life, to present to the world a style of branding that categorically remains true to the essence and heritage of Islam. Following this, the on-going branding challenge will be how to maintain this over time, along with remaining relevant and authentic.

A way in which you can do this is by communicating the heritage of the brand, the values and aspirations of the founders and employees through iterations, and maintaining design style consistency throughout all marketing materials and packaging. You have to be careful of too much repetition, as this will wear your message out; and it has to be more sophisticated than saying, *'I am a Muslim'*, *'Our product is from a Muslim country'*, *'we have a Halal certificate and logo'*, and using the colour green, Arabic calligraphy and geometric designs. Those could be a starting point for your creative thinking, but they may not resonate with consumers when it comes to how they assess aspects of desirability, status, and quality.

You need to study which top brands across sectors have managed to capture the hearts, minds, and purses of consumers. The reality is that if you look at sales and brand rankings, regardless of whether they are targeting Muslims or non-Muslims, many of the top-performing brands are not the ones that are so overtly Islamic in their packaging and messaging. This is where diligence and researching the brands in your respective industry will be critical.

Your research may also lead you to disrupt and shake up the current status quo - if it even exists. For example, if all the brands are using the colour green, then it will be hard for you to become a brand-leader without outspending your competitors, in order to break existing perceptions associating particular brands and colours together.

For example, you produce olive oil, and you've identified that heritage and the country of origin are important. But there are so many existing brands on the market that communicate using their country name and how long ago they were established. After some brainstorming surrounding what words and attributes are liked with Islam, and observing how consumers use olive oil, you decide to call your brand of olive oil *Sahabah*. *Sahabah* is an Arabic word meaning companions, and more specifically in the context of Islam, companions of the Prophet Muhammad. The *sahabah* narrated the opinions and practices of the Prophet Muhammad. You want to communicate that your olive oil is the perfect ingredient and accompaniment to a number of recipes. Therefore, you arrive at the following brand and slogans:

Sahabah – your best friend.

Sahabah – the perfect companion to your meal.

Sahabah – the olive oil you can rely on.

However, if you want to build a copy-cat brand, and the various Muslim colas spring to mind here, then choosing the same colour as the brand leader makes sense. The challenge with copycat brands though is that you won't be able to command a comparable retail price, which means less money back into the business, and your product life cycle may be a lot shorter - through less funds, or the novelty of your brand wearing off.

Slightly off topic: what I find interesting is the trend in

football teams of changing their secondary away-kit colours each season. Whilst you might think that this is just a marketing ploy designed to increase kit sales, and there's nothing wrong with that, it also refreshes image perceptions and sparks interest. If you apply the same thinking to Halal product design, you may want to think about how you can use secondary colours and then change them from time to time, in order to create renewed curiosity and grab attention. For this to work though, you need the anchor of a strong brand and logo that consumers can recognise and are familiar with.

If we think about Nike, Adidas, and Puma logos for example, then we don't associate them with one particular colour, which can be attractive if you want more colour flexibility. This approach works especially if you consider that consumers, unconsciously, can be influenced by their relationship with colours linked to culture, or for example the colours of their national flag. From this you'll get a sense that it may be important for you to change brand and packaging colours for particular countries.

When we compare the logos and packaging of many Halal brands, they tend to use standard fonts in Arabic or English that you or I can get from our keyboards. Based upon my own experiences and having been an examiner for several PhDs and journal papers on this topic, I think that some of the time this lack of creativity is because small business owners don't understand the power of brand design fully; or larger companies underestimate how much Islamic aesthetics can influence Muslim consumers differently; or in both cases they haven't wanted to invest time and money into using experts - and therefore cut corners.

Similarly, if Halal brands attempt to do something more sophisticated by using Arabic calligraphy, many create calligraphic logos that follow similar rules, which then end up making them look too alike. This is especially telling, as many people regardless of their Arabic language proficiency cannot read the Arabic, as it is very stylised - and so their relationship with the logo is based more on recognising the shapes than the actual words. I have seen a number of tear-drop logos which look very similar to that of the news station Al Jazeera, which may be intentional, but it is debatable whether it benefits Al Jazeera more than the other brand. Therefore, it makes sense to find a specialist designer who can create typographically and pictographically unique images that come together cohesively.

You should also consider how many different languages you are going to use in your logo and slogan, outside of the necessary legal requirements for listing ingredients in the local language. There is no one rule of thumb here and some brands have broken rules - perhaps the most iconic being Audi's 'Vorsprung durch Technik' advertising slogan, used in a UK English speaking market as a way of communicating German quality, efficiency, progress and technology, in a way that British consumers interpreted as being superior to their local brands.

The Halal market in some ways is in its infancy, and I say this because there is evidence to suggest that consumers are split in their interpretation of this Arabic word. Regardless of their religious beliefs, some see Halal as a mark of added quality, but sadly others perceive that it may mean the exact opposite. If Halal brands are to rise, then more work has to be done to raise standards and reinforce the positive attributes associated with Halal - but you can't just tell and sell, you have to show and prove.

Another mistake that I see made by some designers is that they try to incorporate too many words into a logo. It may look great when it's displayed on a massive computer monitor or PowerPoint projection, but most of the time, your logo will appear no bigger than the size of your finger nail on a package, flyer, business card, web page, or smart phone screen. So take the time to check your logo at the different sizes that you intend to use it and double check that it remains crisp when it's printed or embroidered at these sizes.

Also, in your analysis, be careful to distinguish between your intangible branding and marketing elements, from those tangible aspects of products and services. Some products like food and trainers, for example, have not needed to make product changes or improvements - simply improving the packaging and brand building have in fact had a greater influence on sales, price and brand equity.

A basic rule of marketing and consumer behaviour is that you are aiming to elicit a process within consumers of generating: *Attention, Interest, Desire, Action* (A.I.D.A.). The purpose of branding is to simplify, speed up, enhance, and amplify this process. So, take some time to focus on the language and messaging aspects and how you are going to share your story.

FLEXIBILITY IN LANGUAGE AND STYLE

These all point to needing more than just the sort of language instruction that you would receive in most traditional language classes. The timing, slang, marketing, branding, broadcasting, public relations, word of mouth, and 'likes' are all key also. We are learning languages within languages, the marketing of language, and the language of marketing. So, could we see a time when marketing appears as a

1 DON'T SEGMENT SIMPLY ACCORDING TO MUSLIM AND NON-MUSLIM

2 FOCUS ON UNDERSTANDING INDIVIDUAL NEEDS FIRST

3 IDENTIFY CLUSTERS OF INTEREST

4 SEE WORDS, IMAGES, COLOURS AND OBJECTS AS COMMUNICATION TOOLS

5 DEVELOP A BRAND LANGUAGE STYLE AND TONE

6 SHOW HOW YOUR BRAND SATISFIES CONSUMER NEEDS AND WANTS

7 EMBED YOUR BRAND IN STORIES

8 MAKE YOUR BRAND MESSAGE RELEVANT TO COMMUNITIES

9 CELEBRATE AND EMBODY STAFF DIVERSITY THROUGH YOUR BRAND

10 ENCOURAGE BRAND PARTICIPATION

11 CREATE A FEELING THAT YOUR BRAND HAS SOCIAL CURRENCY

12 REMIND, TO DRIVE FAMILIARITY AND MEMORABILITY

course in more degrees, like science or history?

Also, building trust appears to be taking a different path. Think about arranging to meet your friends. Before, you arranged to meet and that was that – your unchanging word was enough to demonstrate your commitment and valued friendship. You only called your friend again (on and to a landline) if you couldn't make it - well before the time. Now accepting change forms stronger bonds. We SMS, Facebook, or WhatsApp our friends, and frequently more than one person at the same time and it doesn't stop there – the experiential countdown begins. Texts punctuate the build-up to the meeting... when you are leaving... you're on the way... you share travel updates... and especially if you live in a city like Jakarta, apologies for being late (or ridiculously early) due to traffic. Perhaps this is also why Indonesia has been branded the most Twitter and Facebook friendly nation on the planet - with a higher proportion of Indonesian internet users signing up to Twitter than in any other country. With hyper-communication, much more is up for revision and change translates into choice.

But I think it's more than that – these texts are also used to share jokes, photos, the moment and any random thoughts, which cement those ties of kinship. So whilst our behavioural patterns have changed, that doesn't necessarily mean that the trust has gone - because we check and reassure through more frequent communication. We have platforms that are encouraging us to share more and to do so while things are happening.

BRAND-DRIVEN MARKETING - THE NEW CORE SKILL FOR ALL?

As branded offerings are so important in every day living to consumers, they are an essential component to creating a distinct and profitable business, and therefore such a basic function of human existence, what can we do to promote them more - through marketing? If marketing traditionally has been all about serving or even creating needs and wants: do we still approach these activities in the same way today, and with Halal in the mix what effect does that have?

Promoting branded commodities now is more about meaning-making, communal communicating, and social transactions – instead of just simply commerce. By that what I mean is the products, services and experiences that we pay for have a greater value than their intrinsic functionality. A burger isn't just a source of nutrition, and a headscarf isn't just about covering your hair. They make you feel a certain way and send signals to others, which we all decode and attribute greater meaning to.

Also, with so much information and so much competition: Brands and Marketing Communications have become silver bullets that pierce through all of the noise.

I want to introduce you to a series of models, pointers and key themes that I would argue all businesses and professionals, regardless of their sector and job title, have to acquaint themselves with – if you are going to compete, stand out, and succeed.

SEEDING MARKETING

It took Business and Management academics and practitioners, spearheaded by those with marketing leanings, to champion a wave of better acronyms and shorthand easy-to-remember memory jogging terms to add structures and processes to the way that we do business. There are now lists of them:

- 4P's [Product, Price, Place, Promotion]
- SWOT [Strength, Weaknesses, Opportunities, Threats]
- PESTLE [Political, Economic, Social Technological, Legal, Environmental],
- SMART [Specific, Measurable, Achievable, Realistic, Timely]

…and many more. In this book you will see that I have added a few more to your deck of trump cards. So is marketing all about a new wave of producing and packaging anything and everything better?

It would be a mistake to assume that marketing, as we know it, is a fairly modern phenomenon. *Marketing* as a noun and verb is relatively new, as is its study as a separate subject discipline with rapidly expanding specialisms. Texts do place Marketing's origins unsurprisingly within the paradigm of a market, which is governed by constructs outlining economic transactions and exchanges; and the production, distribution, and consumption of goods and services. The picture painted is one of merchants in a marketplace.

However, with the advent of the technological revolution, and the subsequent information and social ages, marketing thinking and historical reflections are moving beyond the initial arguments of marketing being the progeny of the industrial and technological revolutions of the 18th and 19th centuries.

From other perspectives: are marketers still, or have they ever been part of a merchant social class, similar to the one that emerged during the Tokugawa period of Japan? Or, are we members of a Hellenic diaspora? Or… could a case be made for marketing being a basic facet of human existence, in the domain of all who interact?

SCIENCE AND MARKETING OR A MARKETING SCIENCE?

Adding to the debate, I'd like to draw from an interesting piece of cross-disciplinary research. Several years ago, I spoke with academics Beth DuFault and James McAlexander when they presented their research findings at a conference on Consumer Culture Theory, held at Oxford Saïd Business School.

DuFault and McAlexander write that:
"By researching primary source documents, we demonstrate that Newtonian science and the birth of what we now know as the scientific method itself achieved acceptance, in part, owing to the activities of Isaac Newton and his advocates that can be best described as marketing. The successful diffusion of the Newtonian scientific belief system was influenced by marketing activities that included promotion, sales of representative and demonstrative products, and publicity. These marketing activities worked to build the equity of the Newtonian brand and to overcome the competitive offerings of the time."

So, I return to the introduction of this chapter to reinforce my position that Branding and promotional activities, known as Marketing Communications are so important and such a basic function of human existence that shape how we communicate, remember and gain a competitive advantage.

To some, reading that Isaac Newton seemed to fare well without any formal marketing training and qualifications will be good news. Also, if we put aside for one minute terms or naming and instead look at definition meanings, or the 'doing' side of the equation – it would appear that Newton was someone who valued, understood and practiced brand-driven marketing.

Furthermore, imagining what life would be like for Newton if he were around today. It is likely that: he would receive media training, hire a public relations agency and agent, and have his own television documentary series. He'd keep a blog and tweet; and launch a social media campaign - uploading content on Facebook, Instagram, Twitter, LinkedIn, YouTube, Snapchat, iTunesU, TED, Pinterest infographics, Medium, SlideShare and other social media platforms. Well based upon his previous track record, relative to now, it's more than likely that Newton would actually be doing much more.

Similarly, if we look at UK particle physicist, television presenter, and former chart-topping musician Professor Brian Cox: we have another example of great integrated marketing. In what has been termed the 'Brian Cox effect', Manchester University (where Cox lectures in quantum mechanics and relativity) increased their A-Level entry requirements onto Physics undergraduate degrees to A*A*A; which is the highest entry threshold for any course in Britain - higher than Oxford, Cambridge, Durham, and Imperial College London. The number of students taking physics in Britain doubled in eight years, bucking the trend for a dropping demand for higher education, with the introduction of tuition fees. Also, when Manchester University raised their entry requirements, there was a further surge in applications.

These two examples are great antidotes to cynical rhetorical questions challenging the value and need for marketing; often inferring that marketing is about making people want things they don't need or want, and transforming people into mindless objects.

However, these examples still only suggest that marketing is a vocation or tool; but not necessarily weighty enough to shoulder scholasticism or yield erudition – or in simple terms, greater knowledge on how humans think, feel, and do, and what it means to be human. I say this because the focus of these two scientists was not marketing, but physics.

I am going to argue that marketing, as we understand and frame it today, actually had to be present from the start of scientific experimentation – as a competitive and intended form of communicative transactional response to a variety of internal and external factors. Basically, you can't do science, continue to do science, contribute towards scientific understanding, change perceptions, knowledge and understanding, and claim those findings - without sharing, defending and claiming your ideas. Competition is a key component of marketing and its stellar scholars and practitioners treat now marketing as a science.

Marketing thought and practice is increasingly drawing from art, cultural anthropology, engineering, linguistics, literature, philosophy, psychology, and sociology. Literature searches, marketing curricula, and marketing professionals' CVs are evidence of this. These could, in part, be a response to increased competition and complexity, and the greater significance and importance of communication and branding – which are happening en masse and on such a scale that they necessitate greater nuanced and sophisticated engineering and control mechanisms.

With these developments there is an argument for uprooting the reported origins of marketing, and replanting them within the ancestry of speech, which is 100,000 years old; and the birth of symbols, some 30,000 years ago. Alongside this, instead, I am advocating the use of more anthropological theories of value and behavioural economics, which are much broader, and understood within the context of culturally defined values - as social constructs. Here, value is judged according to 'meaning-making'.

So, as we are in the business of meaning-making, communal communicating, and social exchanges, so too dawns an age of embracing and celebrating more human traits. This is marketing that accepts and harnesses the paradoxical, oxymoronic, allegorical, metaphorical, and esoteric tensions in culture, emotion and spirituality. Humans are curious and intriguing creatures!

Therefore, what I am saying is that if you want to do Halal, then you have to do brand-driven marketing, and you shouldn't view it as being anything new or negative – this is what humans do!

SOME PEOPLE TALK RELIGION, WHEN THEY'RE ACTUALLY THINKING RACE

PROMOTIONAL ACTIVITIES – FROM A-TO-G

So, where do we go from here? The 4P's of marketing are a well-established and enshrined set of tools, which have maintained their position. But in doing so, they are constantly being reinterpreted, repositioned and extended, in order to maintain their fit with changing geographies. In the 2010 book, *Marketing 3.0*, by Kotler, Kartajaya and Setiawan, they broke with convention - outlining phases of development according to:

- Marketing 1.0 (product-based)
- 2.0 (consumer-based)
- and now 3.0 (customers as multidimensional, values-driven people, and potential collaborators).

When I spoke to them, interestingly some of their inspiration for *Marketing 3.0*, which they describe as the *Human Spirit*, was taken from values and practices that they saw outlined in Islam. Especially fascinating and significant as none of the authors are Muslim.

In support of their work and in response to the 21st century advancements in connectivity, technology, commoditization, personalization, cross-culturalism, hybridization, virtual socialization: I wanted to focus on the process of structuring and engineering a more human approach to marketing.

The following set of guiding principles are offered regardless of the market, or marketing function; and can be applied on a macro, mezzo, or micro level. They are also equally applicable to the marketing of products, services, organizations, ideas, individuals, collectives, causes, and nations. In-keeping with the spirit of marketing, I've created a marketing model whose letters also market the model.

Marketers, their offerings, and promotional activities have to be: Articulate, Branded, Credible, Dedicated, Emotional, Functional, and Giving [Figure]. If these can be executed and conveyed successfully, then there is a greater likelihood of target audiences mirroring these activities, leading to greater synergy and collective fulfilment. To this end, the model can be used as an interrogative checklist to establish *what*, *how* and *where* there is evidence of these activities.

Articulate: The ability to speak fluently and coherently, injecting ideas, information, and feelings - in the right way, at the right time, and in the right place. 'Speaking' is more than transmitting words and data with pitch, pace and tone; or initiating and responding to communication – it also encompasses the concept of de-

ploying symbols, gestures, and objects. Your products, services, systems, employees and consumers all have to 'speak' to each other – internally and externally. Articulation is also the ability to break things down, join them together and manipulate them in a coordinated yet 'fuzzy' way. This idea of eliciting *Gestaltism* advocates that, *"the whole is other than the sum parts"* – there is a bigger picture being painted.

Branded: Labelling, claiming, packaging, and joining things together – under one shared interpretive identity. These are the: commodities, services, activities, ideas, communication, individuals and collectives – all in a unified way that is easier to understand, locate, and share.

Credible: A readiness and ability to impart authentic, believable, trust-evoking, and definitive propositions and communications. This is very much an active and collaborative process. The greater the credibility, the greater the latent and current social capital; and more time people are likely to spend engaging, over a longer horizon.

Dedicated: A conscientious, planned, strategic, and consolidated commitment to delivery; driven by a desire for stability and excellence – manifest in employees and stakeholders; and the tangibles and intangibles that they produce.

Emotional: Compassion and an acceptance of human spirit. Now more than ever Marketing is driven by sociocultural exchanges – and many of these created networks are creative, nuanced, and perishable emotional constructs. These activities cannot be rationalized or controlled completely - and if too much rationalization and control is exerted in the absence of emotion, then there is a risk of: destroying bonds and networks, a rejection of power, or simply missing the point and the bigger picture.

Functional: Knowing, having, and serving a defined, but flexible purpose - with syncretism and synchrony. This is the bedrock for enhancing emotion, maintaining relevance, value, salience, top of the mind awareness, and sustained relative advantage. If your branded offerings have no current, revolutionary, and evolutionary role, then their functionality will start to diminish. I'd also like to make the point that brand and object functionality in a consumer society are frequently symbolic and aspirational too. So, what they mean to you, how

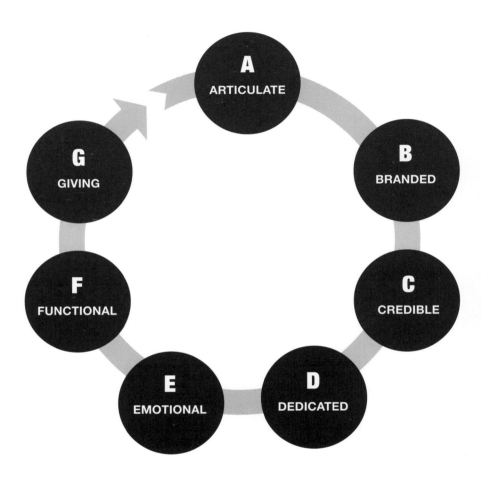

Figure: Attributes and guiding principles of 21st century Marketing: A-to-G

they make you feel, and what they communicate to others are just as important - which therefore make these additional factors components of functionality too. This is way of thinking that argues objects and experiences help people to formulate their identities.

Giving: A mind-set of giving and not necessarily giving to receive straight away, or in the form of a straightforward transactional exchange. But instead, giving with the hope that you will receive something(s), somewhere, from wide sources, and eventually to a sum value greater than your investments. Taking a more altruistic long-tail approach, the importance of the individual, niches, creativity and innovation, new markets, and the less affluent are embraced and nurtured - rather than being overlooked or shut down.

I-MARKETING

So, 21st century marketing is the dawn of an age that embraces and celebrates more human traits - beyond simple industrialisation, commerce and structuralism. Financial and economic transactions are the culmination of human transactions in the widest sense. These begin and end with transactional exchanges of thoughts, emotions, experiences and social activities. In addition, more non-marketing professionals are increasingly collaborating with consumers – each of whom are becoming integral parts of this movement and behaving like marketers. I would also add to this that in conjunction with social media, more people see themselves as journalists.

In short – it's complicated out there and we marketers need to mirror that complexity with practical, diverse, layered and integrated propositions. For those of you that have watched the movie *Inception*, then you'll know what I mean. It's about entering dreams and creating dreams within dreams.

Following these guiding principles and the idea of championing cultural imperatives, I would like to drill down further on the role of the individualism within marketing geographies – as collaborative creators, architects, agents and facilitators.

Now individualism might seem like a strange thing to argue for a Muslim community and Halal ecosystem that prides itself on the concept of *ummah* [one community, one family] – but I am a firm believer of attempting to put people first and at the centre of all marketing and branding activities.

The following model presents the attributes, skills and activities of individuals within this marketing landscape: that is how they behave and see themselves – and how we should see and treat them.

'I' as a letter, prefix, and word has been brought to the forefront of our psyches more so than ever in the 21st century – thanks to the Internet, Apple, and our increased expressions of personal opinion and individualism on social media.

And so I feel that presenting an *I-Marketing model* is timely, and mirrors such changes. Furthermore, my use of an 'I' is an attempt to expand its usage beyond the technology sector – as Internet and technology usage have now become intertwined and embedded within all spheres.

So with the blurring of boundaries, partly due to the desires to follow more customer-centric approaches, a wider acceptance of cultural differences, and the social impact of the Internet: I want to reflect the true nature of collaboration in the 21st century – from genesis to its logical culmination.

When I've written previously on the modern phenomenon of branded creativity and creative consumption, I've highlighted the levelling effect of the digital revolution – where access to knowledge capital and social networking has the ability to empower and drive cosmopolitanism. This has led to a change in mind-set amongst corporations – where monetizing audiences occurs through direct and indirect interactions with communities and fostering nurturing dialogues.

In-keeping with the arguments presented in *Marketing 3.0* by Kotler, Kartajaya and Setiawan, and extending them further: I've chosen not to separate the role of individuals into one-way or two-way polar diagrams of the 'marketer' and 'consumer' that you often find.

Instead, I've decoupled roles from formal job titles. Conventional thinking, associated with job titles, suggests that a job is an obligation governed by a formal contract. Within the field of Human Resource Management (HRM), it is widely accepted that psychological contracts fast overtake formal contractual obligations in day-to-day practices. Legally binding contracts tend to feature at the beginning of a relationship and later on when things go wrong.

Therefore in harmony with HRM thinking: marketing is becoming less about the dogma of enshrined definitions and legally defensible positions; and more about socio-cultural psychological contracts of meaning-making and doing. Laws are there to be used through embracing interpretive practises, which refine and set new precedents. If understood and practised fully, collaboration, customization, innovation and ultimately harmonization stand a better chance.

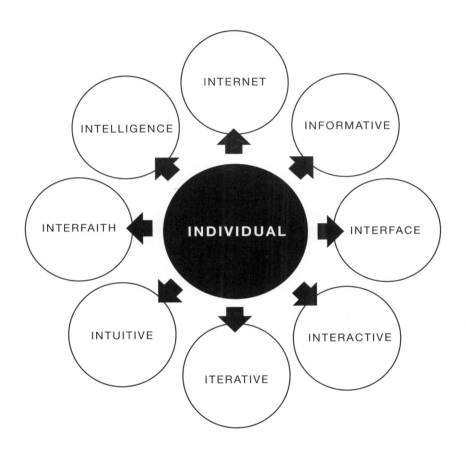

Figure: I-Marketing

I(SLAMIC)-MARKETING

My other intended use of the 'I' is designed to link and reposition the role and understanding of Islam. Islam, for many reasons, is a hot topic in business now and the term *Islamic Marketing* over nearly the past decade has grown in usage.

I am Editor-in-Chief of the *Journal of Islamic Marketing*, which is an international academic journal, so I have seen first hand how many academics are researching and publishing on every facet of marketing related to Islam and Muslim experiences. In fact each year the journal has grown in standing, and we have had to increase the number of papers that we publish each year. Even with these increases, I am still closing journal issues approximately up to one and a half years in advance.

However, having made all these points, I think that it would be wrong to say that Islamic marketing per se is something new. From an Islamic perspective: The best of Islamic marketers is the Prophet Muhammad (peace be upon him); Islamic marketing's origins can be traced back to the Prophet Adam at the start of humanity; and the father of the Abrahamic faiths is the Prophet Ibrahim (peace and blessings on them all).

So this *Islamic prefixing* of marketing in many ways shares parallels with the 'Intel argument' - a processor that's been there running away, with little prominence, until it was more overtly branded, labelled and stuck on the outside of computers with its own jingle.

The Prophet Muhammad (peace be upon him) was a messenger, reformer, and a businessman. He sought to establish new ties based upon a meritocracy - challenging concepts of hierarchy, according to race, age, wealth, class, and tribe. Purification of the self and helping others, were the path to well-being, salvation and enlightenment.

Therefore my argument is that Islamic marketing and Halal Branding will benefit from not only linking back to its rich cultural heritage; but also through creating a new culture of empowered individuals, equipped for the 21st century.

This work should continue to follow in the old traditions of attempting to engage with the wider community and not just marketing to 'them' (Muslim or non-Muslim). Rather, it should not be about 'us' the marketer and 'them' the consumer, and instead it should be about a sense of being together within the same community and even going as far as showing your audience what the market is, what value it serves, and how they can play a valuable part.

Therefore, Islamic marketing and Halal communications shouldn't be isolationist, exclusive, weighed down by technical terms that only a few educated scholars can understand, or settle for being a subset of Marketing. It has to feed into the bigger debate and narrative in a way that can be understood by many types of people regardless of their faith. This is *da'wah* in the truest sense – An Arabic word meaning an invitation to an Islamic way of life.

Furthermore, with Islamic marketing and Halal promotions, the focus should be on the person, not the object. My observations find that much is made about the compliance of products and services, through Halal certification, whilst less can be said about impressing the importance of management issues and the character of individuals.

So for example, truly Islamic finance and Halal offerings should first and foremost start with the professionals - and only then will their products and services remain pure, true and authentic. If the reverse is attempted, then matters are open to abuse or may attract negative attention and questions.

This point, perhaps, is potentially a key contribution that Islamic marketing and Halal can make – especially in supporting the rising agendas of ethics, best practice, sustainability, and social responsibility. Of course, these ideals are not unique to Islam – but Islam has been successful in raising a flag for the importance, role and necessity of faith in business and being interested in individuals' involvement, their opinions, and practices.

So with more consumer-centric, social, collaborative, and relational approaches being called for, I argue that there is an inherent shortfall in many marketing models. Current marketing approaches and models do little to analyse and segment marketers, to the same level and depth as they dissect consumers, or to join the two parties together [marketers and consumers] – and this makes little sense to me.

You will read in mainstream literature that there is the idea of marketing - and then there is marketing management. From an Islamic perspective, the overlap has to be much greater - as marketers in the Halal space, Muslim or non-Muslim, have to practice what they preach, through their consumption in order to achieve the highest levels of consumer trust, reciprocity and resonance. That means that achieving and celebrating staff diversity is a core imperative.

Also, despite Orientalist literature and media stories eroticizing, peculiarizing, and objectifying Muslims - and by extension alienating them: Muslims are not aliens, nor are they a different species. The majority of their lives share a commonality with other groups – more binds them than separates them from 'others'.

Therefore, some have argued that there is no reason why a separate subject discipline should be created and there is little need for specialist books, consultants and agencies that brand themselves as being *Islamic* or *Halal*.

In response, I assert that to paint a veneer over differences would be folly. Rather, a focus should be maintained that details, celebrates, and shares differences on a level playing field and within a bigger picture. Only then can things move forward, in the same way that feminist and race studies have, for example.

However as the Halal landscape today is such a cross-disciplinary one, I believe strongly, that we need teams of experts - which is something that needs to happen, in order to move discussions and activities from being aspirational towards being more transformational and inspirational. Aspirations are great, but they don't grow and sustain markets, and if you don't have subject-specific technical expertise and tools, then serious gaffes can occur. Now, businesses have made supportive noises in this direction, but at times have been resistant to actually dedicate resources to these marketing and branding areas.

You could even go further in saying that it's a defensive response meant to protect existing player's positions and to slow down the positively disruptive arrival of Halal and Muslim participation in the boardrooms and in the malls.

As illustrative examples: it would now seem odious to

suggest that only black musicians can really play the blues; Hip hop is a 'black thing'; you have to be Japanese to practice the martial arts; or the reason that there are fewer female managers is because they are less able. These myths have been debunked. Yet, for a variety of reasons, a greater proportion of erroneous and unproductive myths still exist concerning the understanding of Islam and its faithful - inside and outside of the Muslim community, which are too complicated to do justice within the confines of this book that is designed to help you do Halal Branding.

GENERATION SO WHAT AND WHAT NOW?

Marketers are great at, guess what?.. Marketing! We market products, services, experiences, people, data, concepts, knowledge, ideas – anything we want to, or you ask us to. We're supposed to understand, predict, respond to, engineer, create and manage human Thoughts, Feelings, and Behaviour. At the heart of this is the ability to segment into homogeneous groups.

What I want to explore in this section is what I see as a 'chicken and egg' scenario - of whether groups classified according to generations are:

1. Fabricated, yet convenient, marketing and media speak
2. Actually a true reflection of reality, or

3. A totem that influences how people see themselves, which eventually brings them into conformity?

William Strauss and Neil Howe created the *Strauss-Howe Generational Theory* – which essentially defines social generations according to twenty-year spans that are affected by crises and awakenings. They assume a full natural cycle of four generations, over 80-90 years, mapped along an American history timeline, which they state also holds true in developed nations elsewhere in the world.

Let's look at some of the classifications currently used:

- **Baby Boomers / Generation Me** (born 1943-1960): Prophet Idealists, in a Superpower America, who rejected and redefined traditional values in a period of privilege, afforded by government subsidies.

- **Generation-X / MTV Generation** (born 1961-1981): Nomad Reactionaries, who were part of a Conscious Revolution. They are the latchkey children influenced by Grunge and Hip-Hop music, witnessing increasing divorce rates, and maternal participation in the workforce.

- **Generation-Y / Millennials / Generation Me** (born 1982-2004): Civic Heroes and 'echo boomers' (due to a surge in birth rates), participating in unraveling Culture Wars. They show higher levels than previous generations of: confidence and team-orientation; familiarity with communications, media, technology; and the prospect of facing unemployment.

- **Generation-Z / Post-Millennials / Homeland Generation / iGen** (born 2005-present): Also known as 'The Founders', 'Centennials', or 'Deltas': they are Adaptive Artists and Digital Natives, comfortable with technology and interacting on social media – under the shadow of a Great Recession, War on Terror, and Sustainability push. They are the least likely to believe in the American Dream.

Now you're either reading this looking for which category you fit into, according to the year that you're born in [you conformist], or which definition best describes you [you rebel]. You may even be reading this thinking, *'thanks Prof. I can use these in my next marketing pitch or plan'*. But while you're doing this, I want you to consider some other factors...

How much influence does American history, culture, business, marketing, and branding have on your reality?

Are we really all working to the same generational timeline across the globe? Are we attempting to follow the same timeline and traits - because the inference is that they denote economic development, civilization, and social status? If these do hold true, will they yield the same benefits?

For example, more recently, we have seen talk of there being Muslim Millennials, or Generation-M, who are individuals reported to reconcile *faith* and *modernity*. Perversely, I could argue that modernity is a Western propaganda-laden construct – where in fact Islam brought with it an awakening of disruptive evolutionary and revolutionary standpoints that challenged existing classifiers.

Dereligionization and atheism are also on the rise. Regardless of what part of the world people live in, some may want to acquire the cultural identity of other nations - and religion may or may not be of any significance within that construct, or mutually exclusive. Also, for others if they hail from a nation or family with a Muslim cultural heritage and tradition, faith may simply be taken as a given, and modernity is something that is totally separate or unrelated.

But if you believe in the concept of modernity, my position is that people deal with modernity as it comes, pick and chose from Islam, and their version of Islam, in a way that fits in with their lives, rather than undergoing a process of reconciliation. From my travels to over 40 countries, I see the majority of people taking more lenient positions because of the internet; and in a post 9/11 world, some are simply tired of being casted as the *'other'* - they just want to fit in, love, be loved, and be successful.

Evidence of this can be seen on social media when Muslims win reality shows, cooking competitions, attain positions of power and influence, and win medals and trophies. The perverse reality is that these 'disruptor' Muslims may not have received as much support or approval from the Muslim community as they deserved on the way up - but when they win, those same sceptical Muslims are often quick to claim their successes. Therefore, I think that a lot of behaviour can be explained by the *Band Waggon* effect.

I think the reality is that civilizations see-saw and cultural boundaries are liquid. We see what we want to see, and say what we want to say – and this is largely in the hands of historians and marketers.

So, like the title of this section, the key questions are: *So What? What Now? and What are you going to Do about it?*

I like these classifiers as a starting point. The job of marketing is to make things simpler, easier to understand and more compelling. In many ways, the art of segmentation means walking a tightrope of delivering practical, fruitful and ethical stereotyping which is generalizable.

So if we are to use such generational classifiers, then we have to balance short and long-term objectives. In the short term, people are familiar with them and they lend themselves to international marketing potential. Over the long-term, you're going to see a lag and holes. Different markets won't perform at the same speed or with similar levels of conformity and success.

If we go back to analysis of the Global Islamic Economy, the large and rising numbers of Muslims, and its multi-trillion dollar potential, then you're not going to achieve these targets by looking at clusters of generations in different countries and joining them together. Even on a local level, not all Muslims are going to use your app., visit your restaurant, buy your modest fashion, or utilise an Islamic financial product. Why? Because they congregate around brands, and brands represent and amplify their human and very personal attributes.

But if people are to view your brand as a trusted friend and representative, then still you cannot be everyone's friend, or invite everyone to the party – because it isn't as fun! The best parties create a buzz - supported by strong word-of-mouth, and not everyone can get in. This is one of the mistakes that Halal brands and Muslims often make –

they trumpet that they are for all mankind, they aren't just for Muslims, and they're also for non-Muslims. Not all Muslims want to consume the same things or be associated with certain groups. Be realistic and think about how much budget you have.

So, going back to the whole generation segmentation arguments: the missing parts of these classifiers are the different underpinning and influencing cultural elements. If you look to brands as artifacts and cultural agents: how they are used, when, and what they mean – then you can start to see a clearer picture.

For example, if we go back to the *MTV Generation* and their diet of grunge and hip-hop – what 90's hip-hop means to a black African American audience, with its commentary on the American civil rights movement and references to Islam, generally means something different than it does to white American hip-hop fans.

To a white audience, it may simply be entertainment, or insight into a reality that they can appreciate and empathize with, but never experience fully. Socio-economic figures are evidence of this also. Similarly, black America is different to black elsewhere.

Therefore, my advice would be find a way to track brands and the behaviour linked to those brands – and then (step 2) map them to generations, with the aim of understanding technology and financial spending patterns, and doing so in a dynamic way.

What you will see then is that consumption and consumer behaviour overlaps across generations, regardless of whether they interact with each other. Audiences will also respond at different speeds and to different emotional triggers. What I am describing here is the marrying of Big Data and Thick (qualitative) Data. So, *Get Woke* and welcome to *Generation What Now?!*

ALTERNATIVE WAYS OF SEGMENTING

So for one moment, let's ignore what religion someone is, or what type of Muslim they are – and instead focus on how they *Think, Feel*, and *Do* in everyday life. The following diagram is one that I prepared when working for the Indonesian Ministry of Tourism – where I was tasked with building a Halal Tourism brand, designed to target Muslims from overseas.

Here, I tried to understand why people go on holiday and to Indonesia. Then, I wanted to prioritize why Muslims do and may want to go to Indonesia. When I looked at the tourism experience in this way, it also appeared that some of the things that Muslims look for also appeared to be

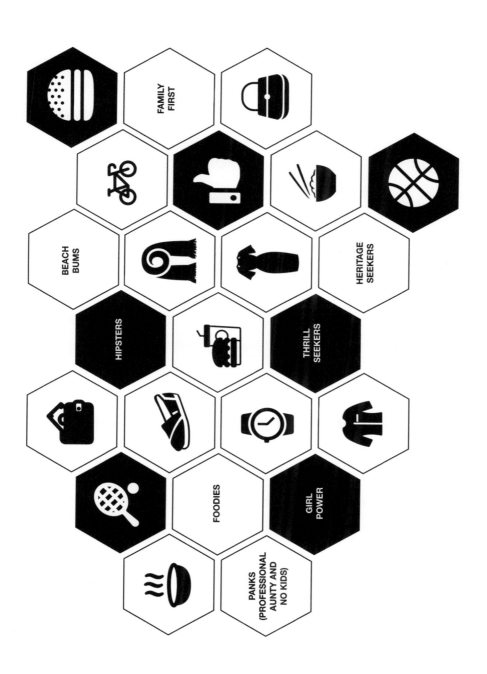

important to families and females travelling alone. However, you should be careful not to conflate family holiday aspirations with those of a group of women travelling – they often want very different things. Also, the reality is that people could fit into more than one of these segments. One day you're a *beach bum,* the next day you're a *thrill seeker.*

Therefore, what I encouraged the government and wider stakeholders to do instead was to focus on the lifestyle and experiential elements - which are championed by the culture, character, values, and hospitality of Indonesian people. Namely, what Halal tourism means to Indonesians, not all Muslims or the religion. Don't worry, those other wider objectives will be achieved if you first focus on what you are directly in control of, own, and can deliver on.

This meant explicitly instructing and encouraging Indonesian stakeholders to share this vision, especially in the face of other perspectives, which are focusing more on defining one unified global Islamic identity, which in some ways is restrictive, encourages divisive competition between nations looking to control the entire concept, and strips Indonesia from it's unique selling proposition. I also impressed that we have to stand strong in separating the global media outlets' thinking away from linking us to stories of terrorism and extremism.

This required more promotional activities that talk to Muslims in a way that resonates with their emotions. There needed to be more proportional representation of Muslims and ethnic groups in advertisements, with iconic Muslim traveller role models from all ethnic groups, looks and colours.

I would argue that for many nations there are too many adverts that show white Westerners holidaying - almost as a seal of approval, acceptability, and quality. This is an exotic fantasy-world that keeps the remnants of colonialism alive. Lots of Muslims travel, and they travel in big groups, and they rely upon a strong word of mouth and referral network, and there aren't many platforms yet that have been able to capitalize on this.

BUILDING A MULTI-LINGUAL AND VISUAL BRAND

The final part of the project was to create a brand image and identity that ties everything together. My mission was to evangelize about how wonderful Indonesia is and to work with the team to create a world-class national branded identity - that links all the tribes, cultures, and wonders together, and contributes towards boosting the Indonesian economy and national brand equity.

At the end of the summer in 2016, I was able to deliver a new brand and logo to signal Indonesia's excellence and

My initial sketched Arabic calligraphy concept

Simplified and reworked into a sister logo

The original main tourism logo

intent in the Halal Tourism space. It uses the Garuda, which is the national symbol of Indonesia, and the one used by the national airline. The Halal Tourism logo is also a piece of calligraphy that reads *Halal* in Arabic, and mirrors the design of the '*Wonderful Indonesia*' tourism logo.

Whilst the case example I've mentioned is in tourism, I think that you should take from this that the same approach would work in any industry sector. For example, I am a big fan of Japanese fashion brand Uniqlo's approach with Hana Tajima's collection, which does something very similar.

Having put in all of this work, an important thing to mention is that brand building takes dedication, iterative and reactive revisions, time, and money. I think that too many Halal brands seek to make the transition from local, to international and then global too quickly and underestimate the resources required.

The Halal space currently receives a disproportionate amount of media attention, which is great news, but I have seen examples of companies chasing media headlines, which fairly soon dry up, and don't necessarily give a true indicator of the real competitive advantage of these Halal offerings.

Halal grabs headlines, but brands build equity. Therefore, one mistake that a company may make is that it over-emphasizes the image attributes linked to Halal explicitly. Initially, people will compare you to other Halal offerings, but ultimately they benchmark you against any brand – because *brand* is a language and currency that people understand.

So to summarize:

1. You have to find a way to be really real, really you, and the best you that you can be
2. Your brand has to reflect and amplify you and what you do
3. You need to discover what Halal means to you and how you choose to express this, in your own way
4. You have to attempt to connect with clusters of real people in a meaningful and authentic way, whether they're employees, clients, or consumers – and maintain those connections
5. Attach everything that you do to objects, images, sounds, experiences, and emotions through association – and claim them under your brand
6. Continue to suck those attributes and experiences into your brand - package them, enhance them and amplify them
7. Your brand has to take things to another level, by expressing them in a far more meaningful and emotive

manner – with less words and explanations

8. That doesn't mean shouting louder, it means increasing your connectivity, relevance, credibility, legitimacy, and attractiveness

9. Think about creating a strong social media footprint and legacy

10. All of this takes planning, strategic thinking, resources, money and time

08

FINAL THOUGHTS & STRATEGIC BRAND WEATHER-PROOFING

CHAPTER EIGHT:
FINAL THOUGHTS AND STRATEGIC BRAND WEATHERPROOFING

When I started my journey in Halal, it was very much a blank piece of paper moment, which was both challenging and exciting. Challenging, because beyond simply placing a logo on products, few had thought about how you could market and brand these offerings differently. Exciting, because here is an opportunity to shake things up and look at new ways of challenging convention.

If the Halal industry is to move forward, and we want to create market-leading brands, then these necessitate new approaches. The best brands have initially studied the rules, then broken some of them, and eventually created new ones. A by-product of this has led to a see-sawing appreciation and appropriation of the English language, consumerism, technology, and contemporary religious practices.

With these observations in mind, this final chapter is a collection of my thoughts that fill in some gaps. The three key areas I will be discussing are:

- Alternative ways that Islamic Finance and Halal can work together and the potential challenges
- How Halal logos and certification could develop a more detailed and robust framework for classifying products, services, and businesses
- New ways in which social media will be changing the way that we approach advertising, branding

and communications.

Also, I've clashed writing styles - which are meant to give you an insight into how my creative thinking, examining future trends, and experimenting with words are important components to my way of approaching Halal and Branding.

For those of you that have sat in agency pitches or read trade press headlines, you will have noticed the increased pressure on copywriters to produce content that resonates with a generation of short-attention spanned social media snackers and browsers. I've found that punchy rhymes and images cut through, spark attention, grab emotions and are easy to remember. Also, it helps to lighten up discussions concerning religion, which still some people are uncomfortable with.

"I flex my PhD in Branding and understanding how the Halal markets are meandering to lands filled with sand and then...Remember how Obama came with karma, but then came the drama - House of Cards brought the beef and played a Trump rump steak and raised the stakes.

White House, white wash, white fence, no offense - it's just fake news, with views we thought were past tense. But as a matter of fact, black lives still matter. Heavy hitters on Black Twitter be keeping the natter. 'Feeling it's half past the hour - to batter those ivory towers, open glass doors to mothers, sisters and women - the blisters shattering ceilings are killing our women. They need their own room in the board-room - organizations can't grow without a womb. If you follow the hymn of your fathers the tune is doom. Being adverse to city diversity will bury your business in a tomb." (Wilson)

So we know that Halal is a rapidly evolving modern phenomenon and there are so many areas ripe for innovation, refinement and market opportunities. We also know that there are a number of Halal hurdles. In this section I will be sharing my thoughts and future predictions. It's meant to be both aspirational and thought-provoking.

REFINING ISLAMIC ECONOMICS 2.0 – A HALAL WEALTH AND KNOWLEDGE ECONOMY

The Islamic Economics caravan is gaining momentum, thanks largely to *'meat and money'* – Halal and Islamic Finance. Both have established themselves firmly as fields of study and practice on a global stage – not only in response to the core needs of Muslim communities, but also by engaging with wider audiences.

Now that the foundations are in place, Halal and Islamic Finance are attempting to do more than respond and react, by addressing more than just basic and core needs. Increasingly, they are spreading across further verticals and horizontals and seeking to innovate and set the agenda.

With this in mind, it seems like a good time to take stock and re-evaluate the fundamentals of what Islamic Economics stands for, and aims to achieve.

This is a period of discovery and development that I am calling Islamic Economics 2.0. My intended use of the term 'two-point-naught' reflects the changes as I see them, which are very similar to those experienced by the World Wide Web - where Web 2.0 signals the advent of interacting, collaborating, dialogue, sharing, democratization, and a shifting of power towards a wider base of stakeholders and consumers.

Furthermore, Web 2.0 is so significant that it is a key environmental factor, which is changing our daily lives, and the way business models and Islamic thought have to be applied.

I propose three phases that outline key concepts which Islamic Economics has to appraise and consolidate – in order to present a transformational and sustainable proposition, with the potential to regenerate and innovate.

Phase One: Defining and Reaffirming the concept of *Rizq*
Risk analysis and management are formal techniques and processes in business - but informally, they are also essential components of human cognitive decision-making in consumption behaviour.

My argument is that with the evolution from the golden age of Muslim trade and commerce, towards banking in Renaissance Italy, and through to today, some key concepts associated with risk were lost in translation – where risk, used to be more about *rizq*.

Rizq, is an Arabic word that means subsistence, possessions, wealth, boon, and blessings. In an Islamic context, *rizq* is that which is of benefit and has been apportioned by God. Depending on the context, *rizq* encompasses money, material wealth, and health - right through to emotional and spiritual well-being. *Allāh*, Arabic for the God of monotheism, is also known by ninety-nine other names – each of which reveals Allah's attributes. One of these names is *Ar-Razzāq*, which linguistically shares the same root as *rizq*. *Ar-Razzāq* means the Provider and Maintainer.

From these we can get a sense of the concept of possessions being both tangible and intangible, and having intrinsic and extrinsic values - which have to be maintained and rendered proactively. Not much difference to conventional economics you may say – however, a key difference in an Islamic system is the consideration and appraisal of possessions beyond transience, towards a longer time-ho-

HALAL TODAY IS A CULTURAL PHENOMENON

rizon towards transcendence.

Within an Islamic economical paradigm, the system is designed to be people-centric and intention-based - with tangible and intangible possessions deployed dynamically. Here, codependent broad and narrow-based interpretations of wealth encourage its free transfer symbiotically.

In doing so, wealth is both managed and created through porous matrices of laws and conditions that allow for osmotic transference.

I use the analogies of symbiosis and osmosis on two levels: because wealth has to permeate the entire social pyramid, and nourish life.

This means that organisations involved in the Global Islamic Economy (GIE) are socially obliged to cater for and reflect the needs, norms and values of surrounding communities. On a basic level, wealth is taken to mean food, shelter, health, justice, companionship, and freedom to worship.

Beyond this, there is a pull to move past zero-sum games and simple transactional exchanges, towards reciprocal wealth creation and meaningful relationships. Furthermore, as wealth in an Islamic context has an added ethereal dimension, then this reframes and elevates the value of certain possessions, commodities and activities into those preferentially that can elevate civilization.

A key challenge that Islamic economics faces today is in the management and mediation of this last point: with such a fluid system of judgment and decision-making, how is the spirit of spirituality maintained, for the greater good, for as many people as possible – and how is wealth created and distributed?

In short, you cannot separate people from commodities and possessions, and vice versa. Furthermore, reciprocity is a cornerstone of Islamic Economics.

Phase Two: The strategic positioning of Islamic Finance and Halal

Currently, Islamic Finance and Halal sit alongside each other, as elements of an Islamic Economy. However, I would like to pose the following question:

Should Islamic Finance underpin Halal, or should Halal govern Islamic Finance?

It makes sense that we should move towards a system where Islamic Finance underwrites all Halal products and services. In doing so, does this mean that Islamic Finance is the genesis of and dictates what is Halal in modern business? If Halal is viewed and used as a logo, supply chain, and certification process, then this paradigm makes sense.

However, Halal has been the undisputed powerhouse driving an Islamic Economic vision - and so such an approach, whilst having inherent value, poses practical and conceptual challenges.

You can't have a Halal product with trace elements of *haram*, but there is an acceptance that there are unavoidable less-desirable elements in Islamic Finance products, which are minimized – and this is why consumers still feel that they have a choice as to whether they should use Islamic finance products or not.

Sadly, I have also encountered a complaint where a mosque application for a Sharia compliant mortgage with a 50% deposit was turned down, but the same bank offered them a conventional mortgage. These stories are so damaging and you can't imagine a Muslim being turned down from purchasing a Halal product and being offered *haram*.

Now that Halal has met the basic needs of Muslims, and as a term resonates strongly with their psyches, more is expected from Halal offerings. This is pulling Halal trade and commerce back towards the essence of what Halal has always been before logos - and that it is *rizq*. Therefore, with such acceptance and successes, would it make more sense to view Islamic Finance as being a component of Halal?

Currently, this second approach would also have similar practical and conceptual challenges.

Phase Three: Halal Brand Building

As the term Halal is being attributed overtly to products and services across a growing number of sectors, it is being interpreted and reminding people in such a way that Halal means more than a logo denoting permissible ingredients, manufacturing processes and transportation.

Often Halal is referred to as a brand. However, my view is that Halal is a term used in a logo – because you can't buy a 'Halal', like you can a Coca Cola, or an iPhone. *JAKIM Malaysian Halal* however is a brand.

A brand is a uniquely named, designed and identifiable proposition, linked to an organization, which can be legally protected. Furthermore, the thing that elevates a brand above and beyond a logo, is its own personal story, folklore, heritage, promise, acceptance, prestige, desirability, and communities.

If we look at Halal from this context then I would argue that more brand development is needed. Halal logos and symbols might be well-recognized, but their brand recognition is less so. Consumers know little about the organizations that issue Halal certification, or can recall their corporate names.

Furthermore, we have to consider whether these Halal brands that are often referred to are actually just Brands with Halal ingredient brands or logos?

Also, are consumers aware of any Brands that are known of as being Halal? Because if there were such brands then you could argue that there is no need for a certified Halal ingredient brand.

Perhaps this is a future area of development for Halal certification bodies – where like supermarkets have been able to create their own branded products, they too could extend their business models and branch into doing the same thing.

Brunei Halal has attempted this with limited success - largely I feel because the nation-branding component introduces an added level of competition and complications.

Nevertheless, there is an argument for this approach ensuring that economic and social capital associated with Halal is preserved within the Muslim community – because if more and more products are certified globally, as is hoped, then it is possible that the majority of goods and services will be outside of Muslim control and ownership.

However, in the short term I think it's essential that Halal branding and certification bodies need more work on the branding and marketing communications side of their activities.

A challenge in all of this then is working out how and what to take from the holistic approach that Halal presents in religious texts - and then fitting, packaging and branding this into a credible proposition, without compromising or undermining its true essence.

If Halal is being moved towards becoming a fully-fledged brand, then following the points I have raised, of creating one brand for all seems like an impossible and perhaps divisive task.

My position is that nations, cultures, regions, and industry sectors should be encouraged to collaborate and create a selection of brands that showcase their brand proposition and promises - with transparency and clarity.

People purchase goods and services with more frequency and loyalty because of the emotional connection and social bonds that they are afforded. Furthermore, this has to be beyond stating ingredient permissibility, or religious textual evidence, which I think Halal propositions and Islamic Finance products rely too heavily on at the moment - as suggested self-evidence necessitating consumer consumption.

TIME FOR A HALAL TRAFFIC LIGHT SYSTEM

A further challenge that Halal faces with a growing number of sectors is that the same certification is being used for each of these industries and varying qualities of offerings.

Where Halal certification is being used for value products, low involvement items, and fast food, then it hampers the ability to create brand equity for other premium, luxury and high involvement goods.

In addition, consumers and single-issue groups have expressed their dissatisfaction, with suggestions that this lowers perceptions as to the true status of Halal and how it should resonate with consumers. Even worse, there are also fears that Muslim consumers' consumption of Halal might leave them open to abuse, as a Halal logo is in fact being used to encourage the unhealthy consumption of items which otherwise would not be purchased.

For example, the rise in fast food consumption, with advertising agency Ogilvy in 2018 citing fried chicken and chips as the favourite meal for 18-24 year old UK Muslims breaking their fast in Ramadan. In 2017, The World Health Organization ranks Qatar, Kuwait, United Arab Emirates, Bahrain, Saudi Arabia, and Libya in the top 20 most obese countries by percentage.

Meanwhile, research from the ONS (Office for National Statistics) finds that young adults in the UK are more likely to be teetotallers than their older counterparts, with more than a quarter of 16-24 year olds abstaining from alcohol consumption, compared to over a fifth of the broader adult population. The UK has seen a sharp increase in dietary, lifestyle, and part-time veganism, with twice as many females than males opting for cosmetics, clothes, and food free from animal products. Personal weight management, animal welfare and environmental concerns are given as reasons for this rise. Whilst the USA ranked at number 19 in the obesity table, the US Department of Agriculture reported that sugar consumption is on the decline in the US, with American consumption of sweeteners at nearly 14% lower than where it was at its peak in 1999.

A halal lifestyle does not have to encourage or require animal product consumption. There are also indications that young Muslims are considering vegan products. Therefore, a challenge for the Halal industry is whether they want to step out of the shadows of focusing on providing animal-based alternatives, towards offering a wider lifestyle choice.

Under the current system, a response could be to restrict Halal certification to offerings that are not just technically permissible. However, I think that this would be overly restrictive and in fact against Qur'anic teachings.

My preference is to take a step towards the creation of levels of Halal certification. Through consultation, bodies could decide what ingredients, additional values, and practices should be rewarded.

So, for example, we could move towards a traffic light system for foods (red/amber/green); and medal system for services (gold/silver/bronze). This I think would alleviate consumer concerns and encourage industry to raise their standards.

Furthermore, it would offer a new sophisticated perspective and contribution to wider industry and consumers as to what Islamic values and practices are.

SOME PEOPLE THINK THEY HAVE A BRAND AND ALL THEY HAVE IS A LOGO

THE BIGGER MARKET PICTURE

I want to take a moment to step back and to share a narrative that I always start my first marketing lecture with to students:

If we look back at the historical idea of a marketplace, or if you visit market stalls today, you can get a sense of the building blocks of marketing, and why they are essential.

When you see market stalls - the stall with:

- The most eye-catching signage
- An attractive display
- A friendly, approachable, and knowledgeable – yet not too pushy stall-holder
- Music or jingle telling you what's on offer and calling you to action
- A steady flow of traffic
- People that look like you, or you admire, or ratify the authenticity of the offerings
- Something that's intriguing
- Something that's familiar
- Something that you've not seen before
- The facility to allow you to examine and try
- Or anything else that makes it stand head and shoulders above the rest

- A process that makes it easy for you to make a swift purchase

…then you are more likely to visit that stall, and consider making a purchase.

Now, some stallholders place themselves side-by-side with their competitors. Others place themselves next to stalls with which they are not in direct product or service competition with, but whom they share a similar outlook and level of quality. Some stallholders choose not to set up in the marketplace at all. They want to catch you near your home, on the road going to the market, or on your way home.

Marketing at its heart is as simple as that. What has become more complicated is that:

- There is much more competition and from more previously held to be unconnected markets
- Benefitting from the effects of marketing requires much more spend
- Branding has an even greater affect per unit cost, and requires even more money
- Advertising, Public Relations, Sponsorship and Events are now activities used to affect pre and post-purchase behaviour
- There are bricks and mortar and pop-up stores which

are spreading out the market – with both positive and negative consequences
- There are Online stores, which make transactions and reaching audiences easier - but raise challenges with regards to how easy it is to convey the messages mentioned earlier in a physical marketplace
- Online is stealing ground on bricks and mortar stores, and mobile is overtaking desktop shopping
- Consumers have not only greater choice, but also a greater voice, more influence and power

...and these present added challenges that not every business is equipped to deal with.

FINDING YOUR HALAL SPACE AND VOICE

I want you now to consider the Halal space. Your Halal Brand has to be able to compete in marketplaces, not just a Halal marketplace, because that is how consumers behave – as they are exposed to everything.

This means that you have to acquire a grounding, knowledge, strategy, and plan that allows you to implement what I call the:

ABCDs of Marketing:

- *Advertising*
- *Branding*

- *Communications*
- *Digital*

...and this is no different than for any other product or service. What changes therefore, is your style, tone, approach, and blend.

Essentially, what you are trying to do is:
- Acquire space – to exist physically, virtually, in the mind and emotions
- Control and maintain that space
- And if you can, make money and time elastic and plastic

What do I mean by elastic and plastic? In order to maximize our three *Pleasure Centres* (Physical, Intellectual, and Spiritual), then you need to be able to make some things happen quicker and make other things last longer.

If you want practical examples of how Muslim businesses find this aspect of business difficult, then I would like to point to the following sectors: processed food, fast food, and modest fashion. Mainstream global businesses find it easy to pivot into Muslim markets, because they have established a market presence, built their brands, and have accrued sufficient equity to be able to invest in developing markets further and brand build more.

So for example, when *Nike* decided to launch hijabs, it wasn't just a branding exercise or 'me too' copy, they:

- Were able to draw from the expertise of athletes and innovate in product design to a degree not achieved previously
- Had existing market and promotional channels that allowed them to roll it out globally
- Have a transferable brand image, identity, personality, and reputation that reinforces their proposition and allows them to charge a premium.

This is why Brand-building has become a core imperative for every unit – whether that's a product, service, nation, or person.

If we look to the field of tourism, it is likely that non-Muslim cities like Bangkok, London, New York, and Tokyo amongst others will similarly grow from strength to strength. This especially will be the case as Muslims want

HALAL BRANDING IS ABOUT HITTING ALL 3 PLEASURE CENTRES:

PHYSICAL, INTELLECTUAL, AND SPIRITUAL

to actualize a basic human aspiration of fitting in. That doesn't mean being the same, but it does mean reducing feelings of alienation and peculiarization.

Therefore, whilst the Muslim cities of Cairo, Istanbul, Marrakech and others might be steeped with more Islamic heritage, sites and artifacts; and Kuala Lumpur and Dubai offer rich cultural Muslim-friendly modern experiences: Muslim consumers will feel a pull towards other non-Muslim destinations with higher social capital, once they are able to cater for and communicate to Muslims with more resonance.

We should also take into account the impacts of infrastructure, economic stability, and Islamophobia.

Following a series of bombings in Turkey, The Guardian[1,2] reported in 2016:

"Antalya, sometimes called 'Turkey's tourism capital', and where 60% of all business relies on the sector, saw a massive drop in revenue as the number of overall arrivals dropped by over 50% in the first eight months of this year. Russian visitors decreased by 95%. Many hotels and restaurants had to make staff redundant, and some did not open their doors at all. More than 30% of hotels in Alanya remained closed this season. Mardin, an ancient hilltop city popular with cultural tour operators, that had seen hotel oc-

cupancy rates of 100% in 2014, is now struggling to attract any tourists at all."

In the Telegraph[3]:

"In a bid to arrest that decline, hotels across the country are offering significant discounts on rooms, with nightly rates at some properties now up to around 70% than they were in 2015. The government has also stepped in by offering loans to hotels and expanding fuel subsidies for airlines, which it hopes will make Turkey a more financially attractive proposition for carriers."

World Travel and Tourism Council president and chief executive, David Scowsill said[4]:

"In the case of London and Madrid [after terrorist attacks], tourism levels returned to normal quite quickly, while countries in the same position as Tunisia and Egypt typically take two to three years to recover. Portugal, Italy, Spain, Malta and Bulgaria are shaping up to be the biggest winners as tourists opt for seemingly safer locations, he added, with each seeing visitor numbers rise by between 20% and 35% so far this year. Thailand is another country where tourism appears to be holding up well, despite a bomb attack on a Bangkok shrine in August 2015 that left 20 people dead. There were a lot of cancellations from China and Korea *in the two months following the attack, but by the end of 2015 inbound tourism had hit record levels."*

So even with greater government intervention and support, we can see that Muslim countries find it more difficult to bounce back - because of the perceived threat and fears, fueled by various media stories.

This is also notwithstanding the fact that if we look at London in 2017 where there have been a spate of acid attacks and hate crimes against Muslims: They are in boroughs that are 71% BAME (Black and Minority Ethnic) and 32% Muslim.

This is perhaps one of the driving factors as to why Halal or Muslim-friendly tourism has increased in Muslim nations, as they are less-likely to be dissuaded by negative media coverage.

However, it's also a reason why Halal Branding is so important. If Muslims do not control their narrative, then others will write the storybooks for them.

FUTURE MARKETING CHALLENGES

Having set the scene, I'd like to finish this chapter with some futurespective pointers as to how you can prepare yourself for branding in this dynamic and intersectional landscape.

"The advertising revolution will not be televised anymore. Smart minds, smart mouths, smart phones, smart thumbs, and smart messaging are the essence of the New School multi-screen scene. The revolution will be devised by advertisers who can act like rappers, and crack stats like mathematicians. The mission: being hip to the pop, enticing consumers with concision, and dropping the right zeitgeist. Learn the art of science, and chart the science of art - engineer unconscious compliance and avoid consumer defiance." (Wilson)

THE OLD SCHOOL DINOSAURS

Traditional approaches to Consumer behaviour study individuals':

- Thoughts (rational)
- Feelings (emotional)
- Actions (behavioural).

Customer segments are classified according to:

- Demographics
- Geographics
- Psychographics
- Behaviourals.

The role of advertising is to elicit a favourable response to a message and enhance desired traits.

SCIENCE FICTION IS FACT

Whilst there's more competition and noise than ever before, the potential to track, engineer consent and verify effectiveness has increased.

What seemed like science fiction in Steven Spielberg's 2002 *Minority Report* film is now science fact. Remember those scenes of consumers walking through malls with personalised real-time messages and triggers. Also, like Tom Cruise's character, we're looking to plug those gaps and report on the minority scenarios – that make or break consumer engagement.

Whilst globalisation has homogenised certain consumption patterns, consumer segments still hold onto nuanced cultural traits that present exponential opportunities if understood, or deal breakers if overlooked.

Globalisation has pulled minority traits into the mainstream; and diversity is a reality for the majority. For example if we take ethnicity, it's no longer skin deep, or merely a demographic trait. In today's markets, ethnicity is more about a state of mind and identifying a shared set of cultural values, which permeate other traits - linked to geographic, psychographic and behavioural segmentation criteria.

NEW SCHOOL CATS

And the marketer-consumer relationship has changed. Consumers are more savvy and sceptical of traditional advertising approaches – acquiescence towards that which interrupts their experience.

This is pulling everyone towards the age of user-generated content - and content which consumers scrutinise for fake news and exaggerated claims. Citizen journalism; co-creation; increased desire for personalised messages; impressing your peers with pimped-out personalised product and service offerings – offering the initiated a hand in the land of personal branding.

It would be a mistake to assume that this means shouting louder. Just like in the story of Goldilocks, there has to be a 'just right' - *right place, right time, and right dose.*

It's about creating a level sophistication, subtlety and secret signalling - to avoid wearing out and advertising alienation. Advertising dinosaurs rub their sores as vloggers soar in popularity - steering peers with their interactivity and matter-of-fact congeniality.

Start to preach, and they zone out or reach for another screen. The television, tablet, smartphone and laptop are on standby – dry advertising eye-candy can stand by as consumers' eyes try and dodge the bland in search for what's

on-demand. The invasive has to make way for the immersive – we're going native. Advertising keyhole surgery.

HAVE YOU GOT GAME?

Old School Marketing and Communications was about
broadcasting and staying 'on topic'. Now it's about sharing
information and insight, in any field, and claiming that space.

Think of it like this: before marketers were archers, firing
arrows towards targets – praying that they pinned down their
prey. Big game hunting is so passé – you can't make that
play. Stop bawling, get in the lane, bring your A-game and
call on the ballers. Now we're playing basketball, volleyball
or squash. It takes several moves, deflections, and willing
opponents if you want to win points, and hopefully the game,
set and match. These passes, reactions, deflections, hits
and rallies are important. Hello immersive advertising.

Get in the groove and think about how much more
fun and engaging the game is when there is a rally. Sure,
you sweat more, but you learn more, grow stronger, and
it draws in the crowds. People remember those rallies
and they become the theatre where people get to show
their personalities and emotions more. Advertising has to
be immersive and experience-driven. Brands are those
anchors and punctuation for advertising signals. Together,

their language and narrative needs to ooze charisma, cool, authenticity and cultural zeitgeists.

BRANDS ARE A FORM OF HUMAN CURRENCY

Brands are the memes that convey and signal, salience and relevance. They are meaning creators, language shapers, and game changers.

This is the age of play and seduction. Brands elicit euphoria and a pull to share.

Amongst all of this we have to uncover what conscious, unconscious, implicit, explicit and tacit factors really make people tick?

These bonds are dynamic, contextual, perishable, nuanced, and as fluid as quicksilver. But can you deliver that silver bullet?

THE BUZZ – TAKING POLLEN AND TURNING IT INTO HONEY

Surfing a trend is cool, but business cats want fishes. Advertising is your rod and marketing oxygen, but fishes live longer if you put them back in the water. Us cats need to get in, swim, and oughta avoid polluting the water. Your brand is the bait. Brand building is about fishing: landing clans that can execute your strategic plan - the storytelling, associating and linking your identity within networks and communities; and then allowing people to respond.

So hold up: maybe we should be like bees? The advertising buzz is about taking pollen and turning it into honey. That's where the money is, honey. Live hives where we change lives and don't just jump to trick chumps into best buys based upon celebrity lies.

If advertising is to resonate and deliver salience, then it has to absorb, collate and rank a series of variables and deliver native, authentic, and culturally centric content.

Establish a hierarchy and consumer decision-making tree, then map this alongside real-time experiences and events, to allow a form of cultural osmosis to occur. Cut through the blur, rub up the static - and test that posit with Socratic questions which embrace fuzzy-logic.

Blend deductive and inductive methods, attempt intuitive trial closes and capture real human experiences and new data points. From this, watch out for the switch - behavioural change can be identified and worked on, so those new touchpoints, pleasure-centres, and pathways can be created.

Understanding and identifying responses are often the end goal of most campaigns – but is this the same as insight? This is only the beginning.

My approach advocates the concept of *surrogacy*. Just like the adoption of a new family member as your own, or the grafting of two different species of plants together – take these analogies as the genesis for some new thinking.

"The end goal is to create an ecosystem where brands and consumers form strong bonds of association, where each embrace adoption with meaning; and there is a culture of both seeking to adopt and being adopted." (Wilson)

The advertising revolution will not be televised anymore. We saw advertising dinosaurs paw over television audiences: no more my brothers and sisters - they're stone cold bored, and we're getting ignored. It's time for smart minds, smart mouths, smart phones, smart thumbs, and smart messaging. Keep them guessing and they'll push the button - this is the age of play and seduction.

MIXED REALITY IN THE MARKETING MIX

How can we connect the global and the local with real-time, responsive, authentic and compelling messages? I've been exploring the progression towards immersive, enhanced, and collaborative experiences that are increasingly being framed and claimed using branding. They sit at the intersection of two axes:

1. Desires for the transient and transcendent,
2. Heritage infused human saliency, against harnessing augmented futurist technology.

These juxtapositions at times pose paradoxical challenges. How can we live for the here and now, and the hereafter? How can we consume a balanced diet of slow and fast culture? Is technology going to turn on its master and take away our purpose in life, jobs, peace of mind, and even pieces of our mind?

For any science fiction fans out there, we're well accustomed to mixed feelings of elation and trepidation associated with technological advancements and the impact on human existence and well-being. Movies like *RoboCop,*

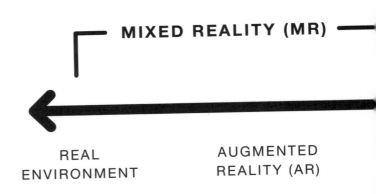

Blade Runner, Minority Report, Total Recall, Surrogates, Ex Machina, A.I. Artificial Intelligence, Gattaca, 1984, Fahrenheit 451 are must-watch films and books where we're on a conveyor belt of life attempting to imitate art, perhaps sooner than you think.

What I have described is our world of mixed-reality, converging around the friendly glow of our smart phones.

But does this mean that we've left the past behind and forgotten our roots? In response, I don't think that we have. Some of our behaviours might have changed, but the drivers remain the same – and this is one of the pitfalls of only focusing on technological innovation at the expense of understanding what makes humans tick.

After reading numerous books on philosophy, psychoanalysis, history, cultural studies and many other disciplines; the answer is actually blindingly simple and obvious. People

AUGMENTED
VIRTUALITY (AV)

VIRTUAL
ENVIRONMENT

DUH, I EXPECT YOU TO BE MUSLIM FRIENDLY!

want love... deep meaningful lasting love. Just like *The Beatles* sang, '*all you need is love...love is all you need*'; and just like Bob Marley asked '*could you be love and be loved*'?

This might seem like a strange thing to ask marketers to reflect on. Whilst we want consumers to love our products and services in order to drive sales, do we do enough to examine all the facets of our marketing activities - from our advertising interruptions, to innovating and changing for the sake of change, right through to our professional conduct, to ensure that this love feeling permeates all of our activities?

As the *Bee Gees* sang, '*how deep is your love*'? Well the best brands achieve a love, which is so deep that they transcend any functional or rational meaning. They suck us into a world of mixed reality, effectively that extends human and product life-cycles to live on in the annals of history. We want to work for and with them as modern tribes.

I argue that the prevailing trends are ones which are not new, but tap into concepts of *nomadism* and *Wabi-sabi* [Japanese for perfect imperfection] - the challenges of nothing in this world lasting forever, not being able to control everything, and nothing being perfect.

The only antidote to fears surrounding these areas are to embrace change, whilst learning from the past. Easier said than done, because success relies upon being able to think several steps ahead about the future, which we never completely know about. Love is that food, medicine, and glue that will carry us forward.

Philosophy aside, what does that mean practically for marketers? If we look at Gen-Z consumers and professionals: brands are empty vehicles for meaning-creating, language-shaping, and game-changing. Social media pulls brands into immersive and dynamic networks, blending Game Theory and psychoanalysis - where sophisticated, contextual and in-group messages signal authenticity and cool.

Cool means presenting a 'face' of an idealised-self that is effortlessly chic and moderated by a touch of tongue-in cheek. B2B and B2C Marketing and technology have to be intuitive, iterative, and authentic. The fastest way to communicate these seems to be through evoking humour, fun, and play that stimulates our intellect.

Plus, Gen-Z sees no separation between a professional and a social self: fulfillment comes from living to work and working to live - but no job is for life, so central to all of this is creating a personal brand, amplified by brand associations, possessions and celebrated experiences; that allow them to move fluidly between careers and consolidate eclectic interests.

Rebellion has taken a twist too: For Gen-Z this means nudging a caravan of followers, rather than the traditional tall-poppy activist approach. The long-tail of indelible social media messages means that Gen-Z rebel smarter and with humorous diplomacy.

Here are four areas that I think marketers should bring into the marketing mix and focus on - in order to capitalize on our complicated and mixed realities:

1. **The smart-thumb business person:** Business is being created and steered through mobile devices – if what you do doesn't work with or translate onto a mobile device, then say goodnight, it's over for you.

2. **Intuitive programmatic messaging:** Your marketing strategy has to be dynamic and multi-dimensional in a way that is predicting, testing, learning, refining and responding in virtually real time. This means working with both big and small data and turning it into something more than just a repository of information. If done properly, you can target one to few, locally, and globally at scale - all at the same time.

3. **Point and get** - like children point at something they want and then try to grab it, consumers will be able

to do more of this with touch screens, multi-screen linked viewing, and inconspicuous hot links on words, pictures, and videos. Regardless of whether you are a luxury brand, FMCG, professional service, or holiday destination – people want to explore and try before they buy tangible and intangible offerings; and to check and chat with whomever they want to along the way.

4. **Feminine communication** - bubbly, constant, supportive and nurturing communication. The more you communicate with relevance and authenticity at the right time, the more you generate intimacy and form intricate networks of interest groups across diverse segments, platforms, and industries. At the center of these conversations are hyper-consumers and communicators who donate their personal brand equity to causes, experiences, and brands.

Now, I am sure that many westerners especially would take issue with my usage of feminine in this context and I am with you on this point. I feel that these stereotypes should be challenged and redefined. However, for large parts of the world these attributes are enshrined in their cultures. Therefore, for marketers there is a marketing imperative to mirror and embrace these cultural lenses - especially when used positively.

However, in fact, I would go further in saying that many of the current cross-cultural business analyses that I discussed in earlier chapters, popularised by academics such as Geert Hofstede with his 6 cultural dimensions, pose added challenges too. One of the six dimensions derived from his factor analysis is: *Masculinity* versus *Femininity*. He defines masculinity as *'a preference in society for achievement, heroism, assertiveness and material rewards for success'*.

With such wide usage of these terms and statistics, it makes it difficult for us to make a full departure from convention. However, I am glad that the Me Too Movement (#MeToo) and campaigns tackling the gender pay gap are picking up steam, and hopefully these will impact on such cultural metrics and thinking. So, within this spirit, my intention is to frame femininity as an attractive, positive, preferential and commercially superior strategic choice.

One final point worth considering is whether we want to strive more towards *unisex* (removal of gender restrictions and de-sexualizing) or *androgyny* (celebrating partly male and female attributes linked to sexuality).

So we are striving for perfection, but it's more complicated than that. In two very similar and yet different ways in history, Arabs and Japanese have shown on their journeys and quests that perfection isn't the be all and end all. It's about being just right - like the Goldilocks story.

In modern Japan, the term *Galapagos* became used to indicate the mistake of innovation for the sake of innovation and change. And I also mentioned that authenticity is the buzzword for all of us - but what does that mean?

For me, it's a connection with nature and an acceptance or even at times celebration of imperfection. Now this doesn't make it easy for us then to establish what resonates, because matching isn't enough; or minimize cognitive dissonance and how that gap is closed.

Therefore, the way to establish understanding is not through driving change and innovation and simply thinking of new ways to do marketing by harnessing technology; but instead by watching and testing behaviour.

This is by looking at the root and core emotional factors

(inside); and how they are manifest (from the outside). That inevitably is going to challenge the economic theory of 'rational man' along the same lines as anthropological and behavioural economists have - and keep us on a journey of trying to establish who are these humans, and clues as to how we can introduce new trends that are largely governed by precarious emotions above all else. My top tip: find love and amplify that emotion wherever and in whatever you can.

SO WHAT OF THE FUTURE?

Be prepared to witness the reigns being taken by a generation of informed, self-mediating, empowered and technologically savvy urbanites. For them, heritage is progressive: they embrace the eradication of hierarchy and knowledge that simply translates to power.

Instead: diverse networks; the sharing and adaptation of information, objects and services; the experiential dimension; actualisation of slow and fast cultural aspirations; and ultimately the positioning of Islam as a 'co-brand' with other spheres of life offer more of a pull.

So perhaps it could be argued that we are coming full-circle to the early golden days – where faiths like Islam, Christianity and Buddhism gifted social mobility and empowerment through structured innovation.

Having said all of this: the one concept, unit and approach that appears to be joining people together is one that creates a sophisticated, compelling, easy to own, and attractive brand.

As a final thought: a good way to build Brand Identities, Personalities and Stories is to learn from comic books and superheroes. Perhaps that's one of the reasons why Americans and the Japanese are so good when it comes to branding.

When you look at Disney, DC, Marvel, manga and anime: and the way that they are able to create stories, characters and alternative hyperrealities that attract generations of people, which transcend boundaries and remain timeless - then you can get a sense of the picture I'm presenting.

What they do is build intriguing out of the ordinary characters, amplifying and enhancing certain traits - to make superhuman, larger than life people and scenarios, and warp reality. Writers also show a backstory of traumas, pain points and struggles that don't break individuals, but make them stronger - giving purpose, bringing hope and inspiring collective good.

Don't forget, there's a large dose of being cool - which you can translate as meaning 'grace under pressure' [actually, the roots of 'cool' academics have traced back to the mentality and emotional mask African slaves developed] - and of course most importantly they stand up to bad guys!

PUT THE SPIRIT IN SPIRITUALITY

Now, before you think I mean that you actually have to create characters in bright costumes and masks, this is not what I am saying - as this you could argue for many sectors and brands would be simplistic, if not crass, childish, and vulgar. These are just exaggerated visual manifestations. You can take the same essence and deliver something much more subtle and effective.

If we relate this back to Halal brands, I labour the same point as I have earlier in the book - many just don't have enough of that X-factor, that emotional pull, aspirational desirability, cool, that stand-out, a superpower, demonstration of a passion for a greater collective good (beyond religious rhetoric and certification logos), and a heartfelt darker side of struggle - harnessed to drive legitimacy, credibility, vulnerability - all of which ultimately are decoded as sealing a stamp of authenticity and value.

If you start to think about it a little deeper, then you will find that the Muslim tradition is full of individuals who have been introduced to you in a very similar way. The disconnect is often that businesses quote or try to link themselves to these historical figures, but aren't able to do so skilfully enough, or they attempt to be these people, and that's something you never can be.

If consumers knew how hard you worked to be in the

Halal space and the negative opposition that you faced - if communicated correctly, this could actually increase your likeability, respect and people's inclination towards being compassionate to your struggle. Of course you can't just tell people, you have to let them into your world, through your eyes - and you have to strive for excellence in character and what you do.

Still today, Muhammad Ali for me is the best example by far of a person (Muslim or non-Muslim) that achieved this and in fact made the leap into becoming a brand. Even though he has passed away, you will notice how many brands still graft him into their creative and communications, in order to bolster their own brands.

So now that you've finished my book, please go out there and enjoy building your brand. It won't happen overnight - it's going to take several years. I'd also recommend dipping in and out of this book several times - because, from experience, over time what you've read will take on different meanings and you will see different things as the puzzle unravels and you enter new stages of development.

Most importantly though: be strategic, experiment, learn to live your brand and make a brand that you love - because if you don't they won't!

So go out there and build one!

ENDNOTES

1.   https://www.theguardian.com/travel/2016/oct/05/turkey-tourism-indus-try-reels-year-to-forget-istanbul-antalya

2.   https://www.theguardian.com/world/2016/jan/16/mediterranean-re-sorts-fall-in-tourism-numbers-due-to-isis-attacks

3.   http://www.telegraph.co.uk/travel/destinations/europe/turkey/articles/cheaper-hotel-rates-in-turkey-as-visitor-numbers-drop/

4.   http://www.travelweekly.co.uk/articles/62837/figures-reveal-impact-of-terrorism-on-tourism-to-muslim-countries

5.   Rohner, R. (1984), "Toward a conception of culture for cross-cultural psychology", Journal of Cross-Cultural Psychology, 15, pp.111-138.

6.   Holden, N. J. (2002), Cross-Cultural Management – A Knowledge Management Perspective, Pearson Education Ltd., Harlow, Essex.

7.   Kroeber, A.L. and Kluckhohn, C. (1952), Culture: A critical review of concepts and definitions, Cambridge, MA: Harvard University Press. Quoted in: Encyclopædia Britannica (2000).

8.   Herskovits, M.J. (1948), Man and his Works: The Science of Cultural Anthropology, New York: Knopf.

9.   Schein, E.W. (1985), Organizational Culture and Leadership, Boston, MA: Harvard Business School Publishing Corpn.

10. Ember, C.R. and Ember, M. (2007), Cultural Anthropology, (12th Ed.), Upper Saddle River, New Jersey: Pearson Education, Inc.

11. Linton, R. (1936), The Study of Man, New York: Appleton-Century-Crofts.

12. Linton, R. (1945), The Cultural Background of Personality, New York: Appleton-Century-Crofts.

13. Usunier, J-C. (2000), Marketing Across Cultures, (3rd Ed.), Harlow, Essex: Prentice Hall Europe.

14. Baudrillard, J. (2005), The System of Objects, London: Verso, New Left Books.

15.   Derrida, J. (2005), The Politics of Friendship, London: Verso, New Left Books.

16.   McCracken, G. (1990a), Culture and Consumption: New Approaches to the Symbolic Character of Consumer Goods and Activities, Bloomington and Indianapolis: Indiana University Press.

17.   McCracken, G. (1990b), Culture and Consumption II: Markets, Meaning and Brand Management, Bloomington and Indianapolis IN: Indiana University Press.

18.   Diderot, D. (1964), "Regrets on Parting with my old dressing gown", in Rameau's Nephew and Other Works by Denis Diderot, [trans.] Jaques Barzun and Ralph H. Bowen, New York: Bobbs-Merrill, pp.309-317.

19.   McCracken, G. (2008), Transformations: Identity Construction in Contemporary Culture, Bloomington and Indianapolis: Indiana University Press.

20.   Gilmore, J.H. and Pine II, B.J. (2007), Authenticity – what consumers really want, Boston, MA: Harvard Business School Press.

21.   McCracken, G. (2009), Chief Cultural Officer, New York: Basic Books.

22.   de Mooij, M. (2011), Consumer Behavior and Culture: Consequences for Global Marketing and Advertising, (2nd Ed.), Thousand Oaks, CA: Sage Publications, Inc.

23.   Miller, D. (1995), "Consumption as the vanguard of history: a polemic by way of an introduction", in Miller, D. (Ed.), Acknowledging Consumption: A Review of New Studies, London: Routledge.

REFERENCES

Academic Scientific Journals

1. Ma, J.W., Yang, Y. & Wilson, J.A.J. (2017), "A window to the ideal self: A study of UK Twitter and Chinese Sina Weibo selfie-takers and the implications for marketers", *Journal of Business Research*, Vol.74, May, pp.139-142.

2. El-Bassiouny, N., Wilson, J.A.J. & Esmat, S. (2017), "An Islamic Macro-marketing Perspective on Sustainability", *Journal of Islamic Marketing*, Vol.8 Iss.2, pp.187-203.

3. Tabari, S., Wilson, J.A.J. & Ingram, H. (2016), "Conceptualising the impact of Culture and Language on Hospitality Service Management", *Worldwide Hospitality and Tourism Themes*, Vol.8 No.1, pp.12-28.

4. Eckhardt, G.M., Wilson, J.A.J. & Belk, R.W. (2015), "Luxury Branding Below the Radar", *Harvard Business Review*, September, pp.26-27.

5. Benton Jr., R., Yip, J., Klein, T., Mittelstaedt, J.D., Peterson, M., Eckhardt, G., Wilson, J.A.J., Maclaran, P., Scott, L., & Schwarzkopf, S. (2015), "Religion & Marketing: Is There a Crisis in the Imagination of Macromarketers?", *Journal of Macromarketing*, Vol.35 Iss.1, pp.149-150.

6. Eckhardt, G.M., Belk, R.W. & Wilson, J.A.J. (2015), "The rise of inconspicuous consumption", *Journal of Marketing Management*, Vol.21 Iss.7-8. pp.807-826.

7. Wilson, J.A.J. (2014), "The Halal phenomenon: An extension or a new paradigm", *Social Business,* Autumn, Vol.4, No.3, pp.255-271(17).

8. Wilson, J.A.J. (2013), "The Trouble with Religiosity constructs", *Journal of Islamic Marketing*, Vol.4 Iss.2.

9. Wilson, J.A.J. (2013), "Bringing the full spectrum and spirit of Muslim culture into scholarship", *Journal of Islamic Marketing*, Vol.4 Iss.1.

10. Sobh, R., Belk, R.W. & Wilson, J.A.J. (2013), "Home and Commercial Hospitality Rituals in Arab Gulf Countries", *Marketing Theory*, December, 13 (4), pp.443-463.

11. Wilson, J.A.J., Belk, R.W., Bamossy, G.J., Sandikci, O., Kartajaya, H.,

Sobh, R., Liu, J. & Scott, L. (2013), "Crescent Marketing, Muslim Geographies and Brand Islam: Reflections from the JIMA Senior Advisory Board", *Journal of Islamic Marketing*, Vol.4 Iss.1, pp.22-50.

12.   Wilson, J.A.J. & Grant, J. (2013), "Islamic Marketing – a challenger to the classical marketing canon?", *Journal of Islamic Marketing*, Vol.4 Iss.1, pp.7-21.

13.   Wilson, J.A.J. & Hollensen, S. (2013), "Assessing the implications on performance when aligning Customer Lifetime Value Calculations with religious faith groups and *After*Lifetime Values – A Socratic elenchus approach", *International Journal of Business Performance Management*, Vol.14 No.1, pp.67-94.

14.   Wilson, J.A.J. (2012), "Charting the rise of the Halal market – tales from the field and looking forward", *Journal of Islamic Marketing*, Vol.3 Iss.3.

15.   Wilson, J.A.J. (2012), "Looking at Islamic Marketing, Branding and Muslim Consumer Behaviour beyond the 7P's – The call for supportive course content and more P's please", *Journal of Islamic Marketing*, Vol.3 Iss.3., pp.212-216.

16.   Wilson, J.A.J. (2012), "The role of Islamic marketing researchers: scribes, oracles, trend spotters – or Thought Leaders? Setting the agenda", *Journal of Islamic Marketing*, Vol.3 Iss.2., pp.104-107.

17.   Wilson, J.A.J. (2012), "The new wave of transformational Islamic Marketing – reflections and definitions", *Journal of Islamic Marketing*, Vol.3 Iss.1., pp.5-11.

18.   Wilson, J.A.J. (2012), "Islamic Leadership: Bedouins in the Boardroom and profiting from Prophethood – Lessons from John Adair", *TMC Academic Journal*, Vol.6 Iss.2, pp.48-62.

19.   Wilson, J.A.J & Liu, J. (2012), "From Laconophilia to 'The Sportan': Balancing Athletic excellence, Sponsorship, Branding and Career prospects", *International Journal of Sport Management and Marketing*, Vol.11 No.1/2, pp.125-142.

20.   Wilson, J.A.J. & Liu, J. (2012), "Surrogate Brands - The pull to adopt and create hybrid identities - via sports merchandise", *International Journal of Sport Management and Marketing*, Vol.11 No.3/4, pp.172-192.

21.   Wilson, J.A.J. (2011), "Refining Islamic Scholarship - through harmonising with postmodern social sciences", *'Ulum Islamiyyah Journal,* Vol.7 Dec., pp.3-10.

22. Wilson, J.A.J. (2011), "New-School Brand Creation and Creativity – lessons from Hip-Hop and the Global Branded Generation", *Journal of Brand Management,* Vol.19 Issue 2, Oct/Nov, pp.91-111.

23. Wilson, J.A.J. & Liu, J. (2011), "The Challenges of Islamic Branding: navigating Emotions and Halal", *Journal of Islamic Marketing,* Vol.2 Iss.1, pp.28-42.

24. Wilson, J.A.J. & Morgan, J.E. (2011), "Friends or Freeloaders? Encouraging Brand Conscience and introducing the concept of emotion-based consumer loss mitigation", *Journal of Brand Management,* Vol.18 No.9, Aug, pp.659-676.

25. Liu, J. & Wilson, J.A.J. (2011), "The impact of Culture and Religion on Leadership and Management Training: A Comparison of Three Continents", *Jurnal Pengurusan*, 33, pp.29-36.

26. Wilson, J.A.J. (2010), "When in Britain, do as the British do – if anyone knows that that means. Multiculturalism in a 'British' university business school", *Multicultural Education and Technology Journal,* Vol.4 Issue 4, pp.220-233.

27. Wilson, J.A.J & Liu, J. (2010), "Shaping the Halal into a brand?", *Journal of Islamic Marketing,* Vol.1 Iss.2., pp.107-123.

28. Wilson, J.A.J. & Hollensen, S. (2010), "Saipa Group, Iran – using strategic brand extensions to build relationships", *Journal of Islamic Marketing,* Vol.1 Iss.2., pp.177-188.

29. Wilson, J.A.J. & Liu, J. (2009), " 'The Pinocchio Effect' – when managing the Brand Creation process, across cultures", *TMC Academic Journal*, Vol. 4(1), pp.45-58.

Academic peer-reviewed Conference Papers

30. Ayad, N.I. & Wilson, J.A.J. (2018), "Exploring What Offensive Advertising is Through the Eyes of Egyptian Millennials: A Viewpoint of Muslim Majority Culture", *Out of (and intro) Africa: Inaugural International Symposium on African Consumer Marketing and Firm Strategies*, 24th May, Morgan State University, Baltimore, Maryland, USA.

31. Benton, R., Geroulis, E.K., Maclaren, P., Peterson, M., Rinallo, D., Speece, M., Stevens, L., & Wilson, J.A.J. (2016), "Religion and Macromarketing", 41st *Macromarketing Conference*, 12th-15th July, Trinity College Business School, Dublin, Ireland.

32.   Wilson, J.A.J. (2015), "Being hip, happy, and halal – more than meat and money", *BRAIS 2015 2ⁿᵈ Annual Conference of the British Association for Islamic Studies,* 13ᵗʰ-15ᵗʰ April, Senate House, University of London.

33.   Wilson, J.A.J & Liu, J. (2014), "Brand Islam and Halal Branding - Challenges and Opportunities", *Academy of Marketing Annual Conference,* July 7ᵗʰ-10ᵗʰ, Bournemouth University, UK.

34.   Wilson, J.A.J., Eckhardt, G.M. & Belk, R.W. (2013) "The rise of inconspicuous consumption", *2013 EACR European Conference of the Association for Consumer Research,* 4ᵗʰ-6ᵗʰ July, IESE Business School, Barcelona, Spain.

35.   Sobh, R., Belk, R., Wilson, J.A.J. & Ginena, K. (2012), "Home and Commercial Hospitality Rituals in Arab Gulf Countries", *43ʳᵈ Association for Consumer Research (ACR) Conference,* 4ᵗʰ-7ᵗʰ October, Vancouver, Canada.

36.   Wilson, J.A.J. & Liu, J. (2011), "Investigating the 'Goldilocks Phenomenon' in Branding: What Size and What Place?", *MIICEMA 2011 Malaysia-Indonesia Conference on Economics, Management & Accounting,* 13ᵗʰ-14ᵗʰ Oct., University of Bengkulu, Indonesia.

37.   Wilson, J.A.J. & Hollensen, S. (2011), "Customer Lifetime and *After-*lifetime value calculations – an Iranian perspective", *Global Islamic Marketing Conference,* Emerald Publishing and UAEU, 20ᵗʰ-22ⁿᵈ March, Park Hyatt, Dubai, UAE.

38.   AlMakrami, A.H. & Wilson, J.A.J. (2011), "Do we really know how one out of four consumers perceives brands?", *Doctoral Consortium, 7ᵗʰ Thought Leaders International Conference in Brand Management,* March 10ᵗʰ–12ᵗʰ, Lugano, Switzerland.

39.   Wilson, J.A.J. (2011), "Mapping cultural change and engineering consent – through social networks and identifying key stakeholders", *The Sixth International Symposium on Public Relations,* 11ᵗʰ-12ᵗʰ January 2011,Tehran, Iran.

40.   Wilson, J.A.J. & AlMakrami, A.H. (2010), "An insight into the brand-conscious Saudi generation of 'Drifters'", *1ˢᵗ International Conference on Islamic Marketing and Branding,* 29ᵗʰ-30ᵗʰ Nov., University of Malaya, Kuala Lumpur.

41.   AlMakrami, A.H. & Wilson, J.A.J. (2010), "A view of Muslim Consumer-Based Brand Equity: The elephant in the room", *1ˢᵗ International Conference on Islamic Marketing and Branding,* 29ᵗʰ-30ᵗʰ Nov., University of Malaya, Kuala Lumpur.

42. Wilson, J.A.J. & Liu, J. (2010), "Why Halal causes brands trouble?", *1st International Conference on Islamic Marketing and Branding*, 29th-30th Nov., University of Malaya, Kuala Lumpur.

43. Wilson, J.A.J. & Liu, J. (2010), "Halal Branding – strategic marketing means, motives and opportunities", MIICEMA 2010 Malaysia-Indonesia International Conference on Economics, Management & Accounting, 25th-26th Nov., National University of Malaysia.

44. Liu, J. & Wilson, J.A.J. (2010), "The impact of Culture and Religion on Leadership and Management Training: A Comparison of Three Continents", *MIICEMA 2010 Malaysia-Indonesia International Conference on Economics, Management & Accounting*, 25th-26th Nov., National University of Malaysia.

45. Wilson, J.A.J. (2010), "A SERQUAL approach to assessing da'wah as a management function", *IC-DAIM: Dawah & Islamic Management – Practice and Prospect*, 23rd-24th Nov., Universiti Sains Islam Malaysia (USIM).

46. Wilson, J.A.J. (2010), "Creating Islamic Marketing and Branding courses for a global business audience", *IC-DAIM: Dawah & Islamic Management – Practice and Prospect*, 23rd-24th Nov., Universiti Sains Islam Malaysia (USIM).

47. Wilson, J.A.J. & Morgan, J.E. (2010), "Friends or Freeloaders? To what degree should brands and consumers entertain the concept of mitigating losses, when relations sour?", *1st International Colloquium on the Consumer-Brand Relationship*, April 23rd–24th, Orlando, USA.

48. Wilson, J.A.J. & Fan, Y. (2010), "Examining the role of external brand stakeholders – a classification through communication mapping", *6th Thought Leaders International Conference in Brand Management*, April 18th–20th , Lugano, Switzerland.

49. Wilson, J.A.J. (2010), "Branding to the Hip-Hop generation", *6th International Colloquium – Academy of Marketing Brand, Identity and Reputation Special Interest Group,* 9th-11th April, ESADE Business School, Barcelona, Spain.

50. Wilson, J.A.J. & Liu, J. (2010), "The Polytheism of Branding: Evaluating brands through their Worship", *ICBM 2010 Second International Conference on Brand Management,* Jan. 8th & 9th, Institute of Management Technology (IMT), Ghaziabad, India.

51. Morgan, J.E. & Wilson, J.A.J. (2010), "A 'Brand' New Friend: Brand Communities in CSR Policy", *ICBM 2010 Second International Conference on Brand Management,* January 8th-9th, Institute of Management

Technology (IMT), Ghaziabad, India.

52. Liu, J., Wilson, J.A.J. & Murray, R.E. (2009), "Leadership and Management Training: Comparing Europe, China and Africa", *The Role of Economic Governance and Leadership in the Development of Africa Conference*, December 8th & 9th, International Leadership Institute, Addis Ababa, Ethiopia.

53. Wilson, J.A.J., Liu, J. & Fan, Y. (2009), "Surrogate Brands - The pull to adopt an 'Other' nation; via sports merchandise", *Academy of Marketing Annual Conference,* July 7th-9th, Leeds Metropolitan University, UK.

Book Chapters and Textbook Cases

54. Wilson, J.A.J. & Liu, J.(2017), "Corporate Brands and Marketing Strategy" [Chapter], in Melewar, T.C., Alwi, S.F.S. & Othman, M.N. (Eds.) (2017), *Islamic Marketing and Branding: Theory and Practice,* Gower.

55. Wilson, J.A.J. (2016), "Psychoanalytical and Brand-driven PR Strategies for a Connected World", *The Little Black Book of PR: Mastering Public Relations in a Changing World,* Petrov K.D. & Wilson, J.A.J. Eds., Skopje, Macedonia: Tri Publishing Centre.

56. Wilson, J.A.J. (2016), "Brand Culture, Halal, and the Critical Islamic imperative", In Singh, J., Dall'Olmo Riley, F. & Blankson, C. (Eds .), *The Routledge Companion to Brand Management*, Routledge.

57. Wilson, J.A.J. & Abdul Rahman, Z. (2014), "Islam, Insurance and Perspectives on Risk", [Chapter 34], in Harrison, T. & Estelami, H. (Eds.) (2014), *Companion to Financial Services Marketing,* Routledge.

58. Wilson, J.A.J. (2014), "Muslim Marketing in a Mainstream Mediascape", *International Halal SME Report Directory,* Volume II, Malaysia.

59. Wilson, J.A.J. (2015), "Brand Islam and the Marketing of Muslim Ethics to a Global Audience" [Chapter 7], in Abbas J. Ali (Ed.) (2015), *Handbook of Research on Islamic Business Ethics,* Edward Elgar Publishing.

60. Wilson, J.A.J. (2013), "Consumer Behaviour as I see it", [Exhibit], in Solomon, M., Bamossy, G., Askegaard, S. & Hogg, M. (2013), *Consumer Behaviour – A European Perspective*, 5th ed., Harlow, Essex: Pearson Higher Education.

61. Wilson, J.A.J. (2011), "The Brand Stakeholder Approach – Broad and Narrow-based views to managing consumer-centric brands", [Chapter], in (2011), *Branding and Sustainable Competitive Advantage: Building Virtual Presence*, Ed. Kapoor, A. and Kulshrestha, C., (Eds.) Hershey,

PA: IGI Global.

62. Wilson, J.A.J. (2010) "Saipa Group – The Iranian car manufacturer seeks a drive to serve", [Case Study], in Hollensen, S. (2010), *Marketing Management: A Relationship Approach*, 2nd ed., Harlow: FT Prentice Hall.

63. Wilson, J.A.J. & Liu, J. (2009), "The Polytheism of Branding: Evaluating brands through their Worship", in Nafees, L., Krishnan, O. and Gore, T. (Eds.), *Brand Research*, Macmillan Publishers India Ltd., New Delhi, pp.207-229.

64. Wilson, J.A.J. (2007), "The portrayal of ethnicity in the media", in *Ethnicity and the Media*, 31st January 2007, London: Westminster Forum Publications.

Industry Reports and Whitepapers

65. Wilson, J.A.J. (2014) thought leader's piece appraising findings in: *Global Islamic Economy Indicator (GIEI) & State of Islamic Economy Report (SGIE) 2014/2015*, Thomson Reuters & DinarStandard.

66. Wilson, J.A.J. (2014) expert thought leader and contributor to: *The Role of Standards Within the Islamic Economy,* Oxford Analytica and the Dubai Islamic Economy Development Centre.

67. Wilson, J.A.J. (2014), "Islamic economy: leap of faith", *Vision - Fresh Perspectives from Dubai,* January, http://vision.ae/en/business/articles/islamic_economy_leap_of_faith

68. Wilson, J.A.J. (2013), "The Halal Value System", *9th World Islamic Economic Forum (WIEF)*, October, PricewaterhouseCoopers (PwC) Malaysia.

69. Wilson, J.A.J. (2013), "Branding the Halal Industry", *Global Islamic Finance Report (GIFR)*, London: Edbiz Consulting.

Thomson Reuters Knowledge Effect, Zawya

70. "Islamic Perspectives on Sustainability", [whitepaper] 20/7/2016.

71. "Islamic Economics 2.0 – Creating a Halal wealth and knowledge economy", [whitepaper] 7/5/2014.

72. "Revisiting the philosophical arguments underpinning Islamic Finance and Halal", [whitepaper] 10/3/2014.

Magazines, Newspapers and Trade Press

73. Guest Columnist: *The Drum*
    "What marketers need to know about the power of Saudi Arabia's new fleet of female drivers", 5th October 2017, "The devil is in the detail: tackling religion and humor in advertising", 6th September 2017

74. *The Guardian Media Network*
    "Brand Islam is fast becoming the new black in marketing terms", 18th February 2014, http://www.theguardian.com/media-network/media-network-blog/2014/feb/18/islamic-economy-marketing-branding

75. *Guest Columnist: BRIC Plus*
    "Brand Propaganda, its Religious Roots, and a Rise from the East?", 7th August 2015

The Huffington Post
http://www.huffingtonpost.co.uk/jonathan-aj-wilson/

76. Street Artist eL Seed Changes Perceptions With Arabic Graffiti

77. Modest Fashion or Fashioning Modesty? HijUp Unveiled at London Fashion Week

78. Tales of Afro Sumo Sheesha Flows in Tokyo

79. Konnichiwa Halal – as Japan opens its arms to Muslims

80. The Dubai 2015 Global Islamic Economy – And What It Will Take to Become a Heavyweight Champion

81. They Want to Know if I Eat Halal Food – Should I Be Worried?

82. Fifty International Experts in Innovation and Marketing Speak to an Audience of 5,000 in Indonesia

83. Global Islamic Economy Summit and World 2020 boost Dubai's Halal Credentials

84. Are Ninjabis the New Punk-Rockers?

85. Ninth World Islamic Economic Forum Comes to a Close – Roundup and Future Prospects

86. Londonistan Opens for Business With the Muslim World: Shari'ah Student Loans and Sukuk (Bonds) to Come

87. Little Islam, Muslim Town, Halal Boulevard, and Arab Spring Sales – in a

city near you

Columnist: Aquila Style Magazine
http://www.aquila-style.com/author/jonathan-wilson/

**Monthly Columnist (2013-2018): The Marketeers
magazine, MarkPlus Inc**